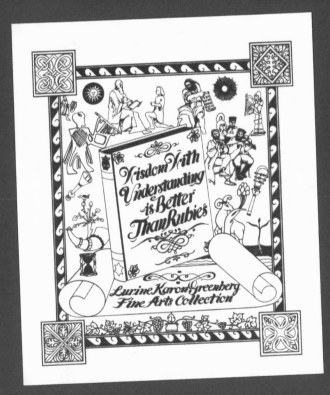

Wisdom With Understanding is Better Than Rubies

Lurine Karon Greenberg
Fine Arts Collection

ARCTIC

BRUCE PARRY
ARCTIC
WITH HUW LEWIS-JONES

CONWAY

For Sam

Text © Bruce Parry and Huw Lewis-Jones, 2011
Volume © Conway, 2011

First published in Great Britain in 2011 by
Conway, an imprint of Anova Books Ltd,
10 Southcombe Street, London W14 0RA
www.anovabooks.com

Produced in association with Endeavour Productions and
Indus Films Ltd, 20 Cathedral Road, Cardiff, Wales CF11 9LJ

BBC logo is a trademark of the British Broadcasting Corporation
and is used under licence. BBC logo © BBC 1996.

A catalogue record for this book is available from the British Library.

10 9 8 7 6 5 4 3 2 1

ISBN 9781844861309

Dr Huw Lewis-Jones is a full-time writer and broadcaster having
previously held curatorial positions at the National Maritime
Museum and Scott Polar Research Institute. He is currently Editorial
Director of the independent publishing company Polarworld.

Editor: Alison Moss
Designer: Georgina Hewitt

Printed on paper supplied by Arctic Paper S.A by L.E.G.O. SpA, Vicenza,
Italy.
The Mills of the Arctic Paper Group are FSC and PEFC certified.
The environmental policy of the Group is to strive through its
operations to promote environmental protection, an efficient
utilization of resources and energy, and sustainable development.

Picture Credits

All photographs, including the film stills on pages 35, 109, 135, 147, 158,
159, 210 copyright Indus Films Ltd, photographed by Zubin Sarosh
(Greenland, Canada, Alaska, Norway and Russia) and Rob Toohey
and Sara Moralioglu (Siberia), apart from the following: Corbis 54-55,
60-61, 68-69, 118-119, 160-161, 194-195, 207, 208-209, 212-213, 228-229,
Aurora Photos 128-129, Visions of the Wild 22-23, 82-83, CGTextures
12-13, 162-163.
Maps by Barking Dog Art from an original concept by Bait.

FSC
www.fsc.org
MIX
Paper from
responsible sources
FSC® C023419

Contents

Introduction
EXPLORING THE NEW ARCTIC

I'm on a journey around the Arctic Circle to discover what the modern world heralds for the Far North. The Arctic is warming faster than anywhere else on Earth and the people who live here are facing unprecedented change. Where some see environmental destruction others see a chance to make money. Over one bright Arctic summer, I embark on a seven-month journey, by boat and bush-plane, truck and skidoo, reindeer and dog-sled. I travel with the last of the Inuit hunters, to understand more about their culture and traditions, which many believe to be disappearing as quickly as the sea ice around them.

In this new Arctic I see resilience and vulnerability, I encounter both optimism and despair. I witness the fine line between life and death in this unforgiving, yet beautiful land. I begin to realize that it's not just an empty space for explorers or opportunists, a destination rich in wildlife and adventure for a new breed of tourists, a laboratory for the natural sciences or an arena of confrontation and conflict but, most important of all, it's a land where people have chosen to make their home.

Of the eight Arctic states of the USA, Canada, Russia, Denmark (Greenland), Iceland, Sweden, Finland and Norway, four million people live within the Arctic Circle, both indigenous groups and settlers from the south. The region is remote and sparsely populated. The huge distances and testing climate are the reason that distinctive Arctic cultures have survived throughout the centuries. I set out to immerse myself in the lives of the Arctic's people – reindeer herders and fur trappers, whalers and fishermen, friends

THIS PAGE: Exploring an ice formation in northern Greenland at the start of my travels.

and families, village elders and shaman guides – to learn more about their daily rituals, to share their hopes and their fears for the future. I meet the new tribes of the Arctic, the scientists mapping the shrinking glaciers, the miners staking new claims, the oil men and entrepreneurs who are making it big. Even as climate change opens up this polar region, I wonder if our minds will expand to recognize the risks that this brings for all of us?

The Arctic is being overwhelmed by what seems an irreversible process of social and environmental change. This means the end of one way of life and the beginning of many others. This is a place which has long been infused with the history of human movement, of transition and upheaval, ambition, danger and desire. One must adapt or die, as it has always been, in this region at the extreme. No longer at the edge of the map, or at the periphery of our interests, the future for this last great wilderness will certainly be very different from its past. Who will be the winners and the losers in the Arctic of the twenty-first century?

THESE PAGES: Can traditional ways of life for Inuit hunters and Sámi herders survive in the modern Arctic? In Greenland, a seal hunter takes aim on the ice; in northern Norway, the reindeer 'migrate' to their winter pastures with the help of a military landing craft.

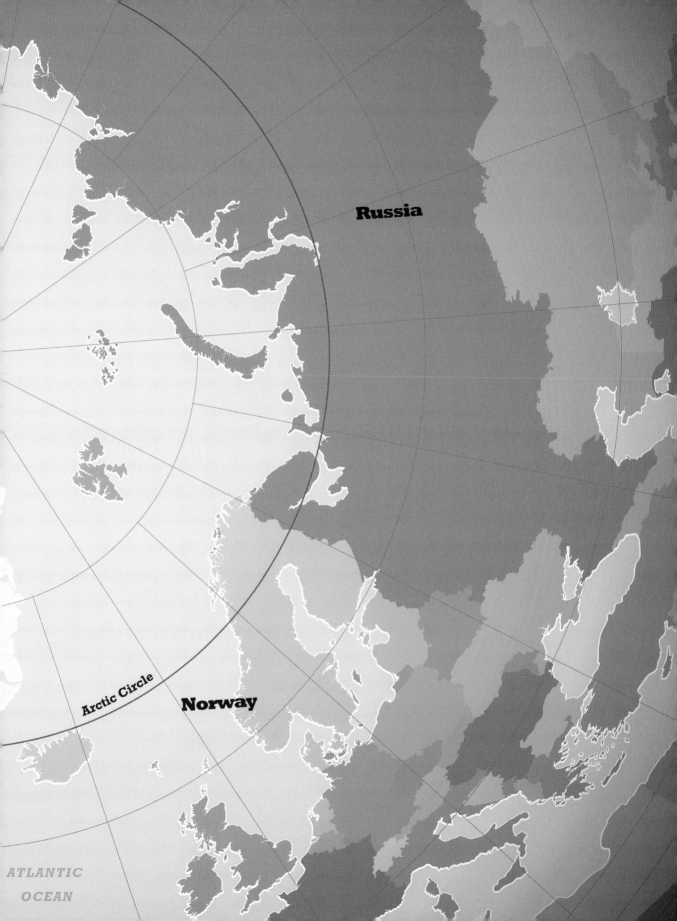

Russia

Arctic Circle   Norway

ATLANTIC
OCEAN

GREENLAND

Greenland
THE LAST HUNTERS

'I don't think I should be sad about my future as a hunter. I just need to adapt to the world as it is now. For me hunting will always be exciting, a challenge.'

Close your eyes and imagine the Arctic as spring approaches. First, in the half-light, loom towering icebergs, the Aurora dances across a midnight sky, the cry of a husky dog, or the crisp hush of snow underfoot. Inevitably your mind is drawn to a solitary figure, an Inuit hunter perhaps, his face just discernable under the frosty brow of his fur hood. He waits patiently beside a hole in the ice, crouched over as if in prayer, listening and watching for the moment a seal may rise. There is romance, maybe a little magic, in this vision of life in a harsh wilderness. There is some truth in this picture too, despite the mad rush of modernity that has so quickly enveloped much of this world. There can be no more iconic a setting to begin my Arctic journey than this, no better place to start my exploration of how moments like these may soon disappear from view.

The Arctic is warming more quickly than anywhere else on Earth. The people who live here are now facing a period of unprecedented change. For a short while, I'm going to travel with some of the tribes of the Arctic – hunters, herders, whalers. But the old ways of life are being replaced by new ones, so I'm also going to work alongside fishermen, miners and oil men to experience the energy, and the anxiety, of these times at first hand. Both the old and the new generation have valid stories, in which I hope we can engage to learn a little more about the human face of change here. My journey begins in the far north of Greenland, home to the last Inuit hunters.

ABOVE: Exhausted after many flights to get here, I'm pleased to be filming once again. Day 1 of my journey – talk about hopeless packing though. I didn't even bring a hat, so thanks for this one, Johnny, the cameraman.

They teach me some of the skills needed to survive in this frozen land. But the outside world is closing in and the hunters face difficult times. Greenland is modernizing fast and exploring new frontiers. Is there a future for hunters in twenty-first century Greenland?

10 APRIL: KANGERLUSSUAQ

It's been almost two years since I last spoke to a camera in earnest. The luck of having a job that allows me enough money to take time off is something I will always be grateful for. During most of the last eighteen months, I've been at home in Ibiza trying to put into practice some of the lessons I've learned on my travels. I've found that time alone has allowed me space to appreciate much of the deeper significance of my experiences with indigenous peoples. But, in a surprising sort of way, I think it may be fair to say that I have changed more as a person in this last year on my own than I did in all my years of travel. For sure, I am less excitable and wide-eyed, maybe I've grown up, which I guess is a television loss but I am more confident and aware generally which I hope will be a plus.

It was only six months ago that I got the call and we began to plan spending time in a number of different nations across the circumpolar North. The stories will be

varied but on the common theme of change. Some will be sad, some uplifting, all I hope of interest. In my previous expedition down the Amazon I was able to look at some of the forces at play in the jungle and to consider how deforestation there has far-reaching implications all over the world. The Arctic is where changes to the global environment are now most keenly felt. Whether recent climate change is wholly man-made or not – and that discussion still rumbles on – it seems to be real and most evident in the North. The Arctic is also where as much as 25 per cent of the world's remaining fossil fuels are reportedly still to be found. This is both alarming and intriguing. Beneath the ice, along the ocean floor, within the forests, sits another generation of non-renewable, dirty and environmentally expensive fuel, waiting to be extracted from the Earth. The stakes are high but the players are the world's biggest. With so much of the global political and economic system orbiting around energy issues, all eyes are looking North right now. Who knows what the future will hold?

Greenland, I've been telling the crew, is a place I vowed never to return to. Of course, it was something first said in jest, and I have no negative sentiments towards any Greenlander, but the last time I was here I was wearing tweeds and fingerless gloves, eating fatty pemmican and pulling a sledge 1,000 kilometres across the ice cap. I was shooting a dramatized film, pretending to be the explorer Robert Falcon Scott.

I was leader of a television team of British re-enactors, trying to simulate his fateful journey to the South Pole. We took to the ice against a group of Norwegian sledge experts, who were gamely playing the part of Amundsen and his successful team. We did atrociously and the Scandinavians beat us by over a month with hardly a bead of sweat dripping from their chiselled jaws. The professionals won hands down. Again.

We were the time-honoured losers, brave, stupid and deliriously happy despite stiff lips and terrible odds. No deathly end-result which met Captain Scott, thankfully. It wasn't Antarctica, but just a small jaunt across this vast Greenlandic ice cap, a feature so immeasurably more impressive than our little trip. In Greenlandic the inland ice is known as *sermersuaq*, 'the great ice', and covering an area of 1.7 million square kilometres it's not hard to see why. Almost 20 per cent of the world's fresh water is locked up here, on this the biggest island on the planet, and the ice sheet contains enough water to raise global sea levels by almost 7 metres. To me that's a staggering statistic when I think of all the lakes and rivers I've seen, including my eight months on the Amazon.

Greenland is also supposedly truly rich in deposits of oil and gas. Mineral seams are revealing themselves beneath the ever-retreating ice. What with the recent changes in governorship, people are beginning to rub their hands in anticipation of what lies underfoot. The advice is strong and diverse and if Greenland can buy off her shackles

from Denmark, Greenlanders can gain what many want, full independence, which will make them the only truly Arctic nation, and a rich one at that. But, as ever, the financial outlay to extract any natural resources will need to come from the outside. So what will the conditions be, from where will the monies come, and what advice will be heard? I suspect the get-rich-quick demands from the USA will be different to the long-term planning solutions proposed by the Scandinavian nations. The choice will be for Greenlanders to make and the fiscal gains could be very high. But what may be lost? As yet I'm not sure but fear a trade-off where nature will surely lose.

The cafeteria at Kangerlussuaq airport is modern and the view spectacular. There was no collection tunnel for our plane so the act of disembarking had everyone don their huge newly bought down parkas, proudly trimmed with their must-have fur muffs. The miners and expedition teams, who probably made up 80 per cent of the full flight, know their equipment, but in the end it wasn't needed. In fact, it was entirely balmy and I ended up in a t-shirt, sitting outside, beginning to put some thoughts down on paper in my travel diary. I've also had some chats with James, my director, about our prospective story lines, which is good. He is on side as ever and will no doubt bring my oversized ideas back into perspective. I'm particularly interested in the indigenous perception of the landscape, the connection with the natural world, both philosophically and literally, as well as their view of the changes taking

THIS PAGE: Dressed in polar bear-skin trousers, I try to get some practice at using the dog whip before we embark on our journey. It's too warm to wear this winter gear for long, but when I do it feels great.

place here. Can they stop the change? Do they want to? What is being lost or gained and what are the repercussions of it all?

It has always amazed me how the Inuit have survived in the North, and like many people I was entranced by the film *Nanook of the North* as a kid. I soon became one of those red-blooded schoolboys, enraptured by tales of polar adventure and exploration: Ernest Shackleton, John Franklin, Douglas Mawson, Captain Scott even. Most of my friends were more into music or football, but for me it was dreaming of adventure in the wilderness. Having pretended to be Scott of the Antarctic last time I was here in Greenland, I began to feel just how stubborn and arrogant my English ancestors were prone to be. Pride, resilience and dogged determination were attributes I idolized as a kid, encouraging me to leave school to join the Royal Marines. I carried adulation for these qualities through to my adult years, but since living with indigenous people around the world I have lately come to question most of them. Scott was a man of his time, a wonderful human who was brave beyond my imagination. He

was presented with some tough situations and made tough decisions, often out of love and kindness, but he was a child of the nineteenth century, and that frustratingly British notion of the superiority of our own way of life. Many past explorers to this Arctic region did not carry empathy for local people in their kit bags. These attitudes are, in some ways, still the products of our repressed cultural history. Those people who fall outside the accepted system are misunderstood by the majority, their voices are rarely heard.

Bizarrely, *Amazon* was on Danish TV only three weeks ago so I'm taking a bit of a minor celebrity hit in the airport, which is flattering, if totally unexpected up here in the North. There were lots of other polar nuts on the flights too, even a French film crew and some polar skiers who saw my Scott antics in *Blizzard*. We have two more hours waiting here before a flight to Ilulissat where the famous Jakobshavn Glacier is retreating so rapidly and dramatically. There we will stay the night before flying to our final destination Qaanaaq. The plan is to go straight out onto the sea ice on a hunting trip where our film will open. The pressure is on. After a couple of years of silence I'd better think of something to say.

14 APRIL: QAANAAQ

I've always been fascinated by hunter–gatherers, but just imagine trying to eke out an existence from all that you can find in a barren, desolate landscape like this. For the Inuit most of those traditions have died away, but amazingly here in the north of Greenland some of that culture is still alive and that's why we've chosen the village of Qaanaaq to start our Arctic odyssey.

Greenland is almost the size of Western Europe. The 56,000 people who live here – roughly the same population as Torquay – are spread out in a few settlements hugging the coast. Qaanaaq in the far northwest is among the most isolated and least developed. I've heard that this is one of the last places in Greenland where people still live by subsistence hunting. A team of local hunters are going to take me out on their next hunting

BELOW: Our first trial run travelling by dogsled on the sea ice – the headmaster and his naughty kids, with one sitting at the back in detention! OVERLEAF: Seals resting on the sea ice.

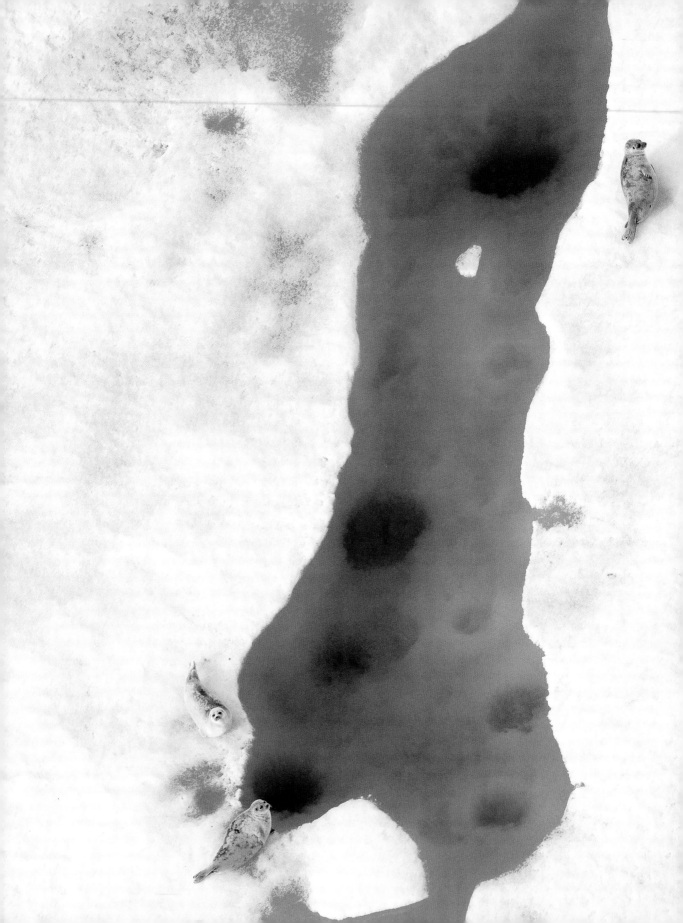

ARCTIC SEA ICE Over the past few decades, the Arctic has warmed at about twice the rate of the rest of the globe. Satellite observations show that the extent of Arctic sea ice has been decreasing since the late 1970s. In 2007 it reduced rapidly in a single year, reaching an all-time low. At the time this dramatic change in the state of the sea ice was widely reported in the international media. Human-induced climate change was explained as the cause and it was suggested that the rate of decline of the summer sea ice was set to increase, possibly uncontrollably, certainly beyond what has been experienced before.

Computer modelling of the Arctic sea ice – by numerous international scientific agencies and major organizations, including most recently by NASA and the UK Met Office Hadley Centre – demonstrates that ice variability recovers from extreme events, and that the 'long-term trend of reduction is robust'. Contrary to initial predictions, some of which suggested ice-free Arctic summers in just ten years time, it is now suggested that the first ice-free summer in the Arctic Ocean may occur some time after 2060. This later estimate is, however, no cause for celebration.

The situation is complicated. We are in an inter-glacial period, the whole world is warming and has done so since the mid-nineteenth century. But it does seem that the rate of the ice loss is accelerating. Warming is enhanced near the sea surface, and over 50 per cent of the thick sea ice that was built up over many winters has now melted and been replaced by thinner ice formed in a single winter, which will melt more quickly the following summer.

Increased absorption of heat from the sun into the ocean is a major contributor to continued sea ice reduction and once this process has started it is difficult to reverse. Warming is amplified as ice retreats. Beyond computer simulations, the fact of the matter on the ground, within communities experiencing changes year-on-year, is that the increased warming here is a troubling reality.

Extensive open water has been observed in the Chukchi Sea, the East Siberian Sea and north of the Barents Sea. Arctic weather systems are also highly variable each year. Prevailing winds greatly affect localized ice patterns, both in extent and thickness. This variability makes it harder to attribute observed trends solely to man-made emissions of greenhouse gases, although there is now a huge amount of data to detect a 'human signal in the thirty-year trend'. What we can be sure of is that the Arctic ice will continue to decline in line with increasing global temperatures. If the rate of global temperature rise increases, then so too will the rate of Arctic sea-ice decline.

What matters most keenly for Inuit hunters is the timing and extent of the sea-ice melt. The breaking of the ice much earlier in the season reduces the safe hunting period, making it more difficult to reach sea mammals found at the ice edge. Ice layers are thinner, unstable and unpredictable, and the dangers of travelling increase. Climate change is already destabilizing other systems in Greenland, including mountain glaciers, the distribution of frozen soils and vegetation, which in turn may affect the health and migration patterns of wildlife, alter nutrient-rich ocean currents and affect the fisheries.

trip. I want to hear about the skills needed to survive up here. But I also want to see how their lives are changing. These men, like 90 per cent of Greenlanders, are Inuit. Travelling by dogsled their ancestors conquered the frozen North from Alaska to Greenland. Just by looking at Mads Ole and Rasmus, my local guides for the next few weeks, I can tell I've come to the right place to learn about Inuit culture. Rasmus says snow is coming, it's too dangerous to hunt so we're going fishing tomorrow instead.

Yet, before we even begin, this evening we have some tragic news from home. Sam Organ, our Executive Producer, has died. As I write this now I can hardly believe it's true. Sam who has held my hand since I started my career, Sam who has been the brains behind all my programmes, has gone, finally overwhelmed by cancer. Before I left England, just a few weeks ago, I was lucky enough to see him at his house, shortly before he was taken to hospital. His last words to me were to get out there, be inquisitive and search out whatever stories interested me. I shall cherish this advice and will do whatever I can to honour his genius and integrity. When he first came to produce *Tribe* he wasn't sure what to make of us all down in Cardiff but after those early days, when it was most certainly business first, we all grew together as a family. He was the perfect counterpoint, offsetting the poetry of Series Producer Steve Robinson, and his meticulous precision reviewing the films was simply the making of the series in

OPPOSITE ABOVE: We are guests at Toku's fishing 'patrol' hut. She is the only female hunter in the whole region.
OPPOSITE BELOW: Toku and Adolph, at pace, show me how it's done. I never saw dear Rasmus move this fast!
BELOW Rasmus prepares the runners on his sledge. At these high latitudes, poorly maintained gear could mean the difference between life and death.

OPPOSITE AND OVERLEAF: We are fishing for halibut and rays. We set out the lines and wait patiently for a few hours. Then I reel in the lines and fish come out thick and fast. We won't go hungry this week!

many ways. We were always so happy to have Sam look over us and in a funny way I think he was proud of us. In fact, man, I'm going to miss you. Sam, you were so brave right to the end, so generous to give your time to us even to the last. I will always remember that.

15 APRIL: QAANAAQ FJORD

Today, with heavy hearts, we begin our first trial run on the sea ice. It's well below freezing, and we're travelling so fast that wind chill is kicking in with a bitter bite. The Arctic novelty wears off after about three minutes. My first time giving pieces to camera in almost two years was not great, what with my fluffed words and 'Johnny the cameraman' slipping on the ice we must have tried ten times to get it right and I still wasn't happy when the hunters began to arrive on their dogsleds. It made me wonder whether I would be better learning lines off a script like most presenters, and I felt ashamed that my rest had done little to improve my memory for information. Sam would have smiled and found a way to encourage me to sort it out.

We arrive at the fishing grounds and get straight to work. We are guests at Toku's fishing hut. It's a tiny wooden shack on sledge runners with her name printed in big letters on the roof like an American police car, sending a message into the sky. The crew sit in there in turns raiding her biscuits, spam and tea – enjoying this simple luxury out on the ice. Toku is half Japanese, the only female hunter in this whole region. She begins by showing me how to catch our lunch. First we need to reopen an existing hole dug in the ice. Using mackerel for bait, the hunters gently lower hooks down through the ice. It's hard to think of a more iconic polar scene than this, a bunch of hunters in furs, stood around a little hole in the ice. Some people might chide that it's a television cliché, but this is real, no fake set up for our cameras. We lower metal kites to draw the hooks out and down below the current. They joke that my gloves will freeze to the line and pull me in, drawn down into the inky water. It doesn't even bear thinking about. Observing how strong the current is just makes the whole notion of going under the ice so much more scary. I've fished all over the world in a number of different ways, but I've never actually stood over the ocean. It feels weird because, of course, beneath us in every direction is the sea. And to my surprise, they tell me there are lots of sharks down there.

We leave the lines out for a few hours and retreat to the warmth of the fishing hut. Mads Ole tells me that snacking is the key to happiness out on the ice. 'We must eat often to keep ourselves warm. Adolph looks like he doesn't eat much but he eats constantly,' he beams, poking his friend in the ribs. I'm growing to like these guys really fast. After a few hours we return to the lines. After just ten minutes working them to the surface, halibut and rays come out thick and fast. We have plenty to keep us warm and keep the dogs happy too.

THIS PAGE: Greenland huskies are believed to have been introduced by the first Inuit settlers a few thousand years ago.

The hounds are big and strong, alert and handsome. Their eyes are bright but there is an edge of wildness about them that keeps me from relaxing fully. These dogs are amazing animals. I've observed the relationship between man and dog in many parts of the world and it's always a happy symbiosis, but nowhere can the dependency be more pronounced than here. Traditional Inuit needed these animals for locomotion as well as for safety and hunting. Vast hunting grounds must be travelled because of the scarcity of game in such latitudes and hunters simply would not be able to cover the distances without massive loss in weight and strength if they did it by foot, let alone carrying all they need to survive in such conditions.

Although snowmobiles have replaced dogsleds across most of the Arctic, the trusty hound is still the preferred mode of transport in northern Greenland. Sledge design has changed little over hundreds of years: they are loosely bound, allowing them to flex as they move over ridges in the ice and they are very light – a good dog team can travel at up to 10 miles an hour. Like the camel to the desert nomad, these Greenland dogs are quite simply the life source to these people and their physiological adaptations to the snow and cold have been harnessed by humans to great effect.

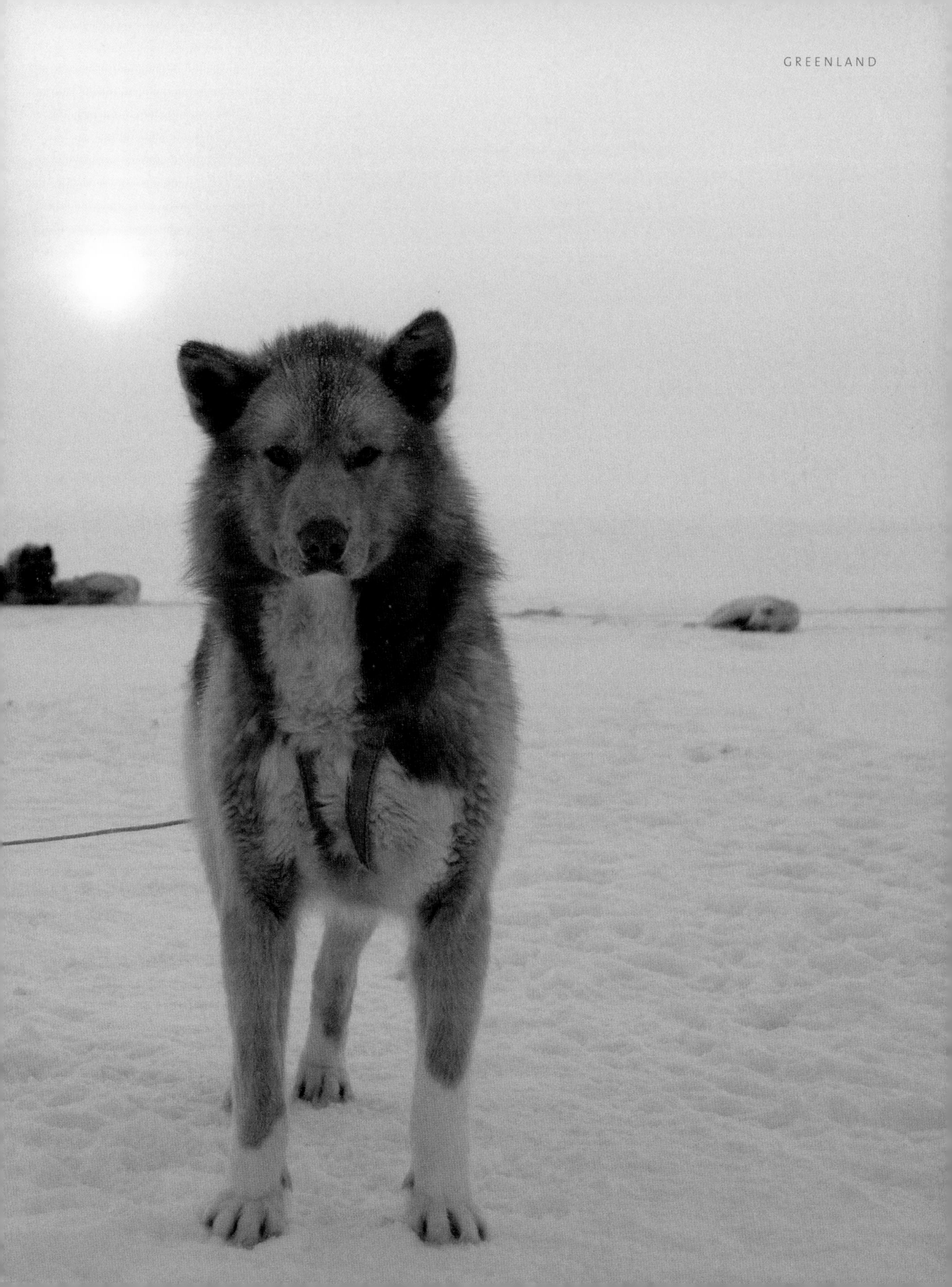

Traditionally it seems the training method is more stick than carrot, but to be fair this is no grassy country estate and these animals are more wolf than poodle. It has become their destiny to be the work animal of the North and, by God, do they work.

16 APRIL: QAANAAQ

Back in the village, Rasmus invites me to his house to meet his family. As I enter, I'm surprised to find a huge black hulk of something sitting on what looks like a roasting dish. No one else seems to give it a second glance. I have to walk sideways to get past it to the small sofa by the heater, where his wife Malia is knitting. She smiles as I sit down beside her. A radio is on in the background, business as usual. A somewhat shy guest, I feel silly asking what the hulk is, but there's no way not to stare at it. Mads Ole is amused by my puzzled look, and he kindly explains it's a chunk of walrus meat, defrosting in the warmth of the living room before he can cut it up to feed to the dogs. I tell him that I keep my dog food in little bags by the larder, but the weak joke falls flat. Rasmus wants to give his dogs a decent feed before our hunt – this amount of meat will feed thirteen or fourteen dogs, he tells me, perhaps enough for two days' travelling. Fatty meat like this is the secret to a sled dog's endurance. It's high in energy and very long lasting.

But animals aren't just a source of meat to the Inuit. Fat, for example, can also be used to coat their boots – *kamiks* – the fat providing a waterproof layer. Rasmus casually passes me a plastic bottle of pungent polar bear fat, and encourages me to oil up a boot. I feel like a new boy, polishing his shoes for his first day at school. I am excited, and a little nervous, to be heading out on the ice. Animal skins and furs are also used to make cold weather clothing. Rasmus wants me to try on his gear for size – polar bear skin trousers and a parka. 'These are the best clothes to wear, even if it's below minus 50°,' he tells me, 'and now I can get a photo of you in them, Bruce. That will be funny!'

With a wheelbarrow full of walrus meat we head off to feed Rasmus's dog team. As we toss out the semi-frozen chunks, they don't even touch the ground. Straight into their mouths, no matter how big the pieces, barely chewing, down it goes. My early nerves aside, I feel that I am beginning to connect with Rasmus, he teases me and he's very gentle. I trust he's a guy I can rely on when we get out there on the ice and I'm thrilled about going away with him.

Next morning it's time to go hunting. Sadly, I've had to give Rasmus back his cold-weather gear but it's mild by Greenland standards, only minus 10, so I should be OK. Malia has come to see Rasmus off. Hunting is dangerous up here, especially in the spring when the sea ice is breaking up. 'When he is away, I try not to worry and try not to think about him too much. This way I keep myself calm. If I keep worrying every time he goes out it will just get worse for me.' We all hug, they share a moment together, and then we head to the sledges.

Greenland dogs are some of the most efficient long-distance runners in the animal world. Feed them walrus blubber and a team can drag a sledge up to a hundred miles a day, and for more than a week at a time. Without them the Inuit would never have colonized so much of the Arctic. But this ancient partnership is almost at an end. There are fewer than forty hunters using dog teams in Qaanaaq. Rasmus and his friends are among the last of their kind. I always have mixed feelings when I set out on a hunt. I take no pleasure from a kill but always experience exhilaration from the chase or stalk. I'm constantly on the verge of becoming vegetarian. Excessive meat consumption is a global problem. The Amazon's main threat is meat eaters. But the start of an Arctic journey is no place to begin a new regime for me. There is nothing else up here. I know I'd rather eat hunted food than farmed food anyway. This is about survival, as it has been for hundreds, if not thousands of years. Traditionally, hunting was everything up here. Without the catch from the hunt there was no life.

The whale, the polar bear, the seal and walrus, provided everything that the people needed. There's very little gathering here, no trees to chop for firewood, even the warmth in your tent or your shelter at night was from the blubber of seals and whales. The clothing and the sledges were traditionally made from animals themselves. So hunting was everything to the original inhabitants of this part of the world, and now, of course, things are different and you can buy stuff in town if you have the cash, but these guys are still hunters. That's what they do, they go out and they feed their families from the food that they get from hunting, so this trip is really important.

ABOVE: Back in the village, Rasmus lets me try on his traditional cold-weather gear, a caribou-skin parka trimmed with fox and polar bear trousers. Traditional or modern, there is no substitute for fur on the ice. Later he takes me out to prepare the dogs for our hunting trip.

THESE PAGES: One of our friends in Qaanaaq comes to say goodbye as we head out onto the ice. Leaving the warmth of the huts, a hug from his daughter sends Paulos on his way.

It's not just a nostalgic look at the past. This is what they are still trying to do today and as a result I really hope we are able to get something meaningful for our film and useful for their table.

Rasmus says it's almost two days' travelling to the walrus hunting grounds so there's not much for me to do but sit back, enjoy the scenery, and try and stay warm. Icebergs are stuck in the sea ice in the distance, appearing like sugar cubes on icing sugar, all glittering like diamonds. I curse myself for having such weak metaphors to mind, when the land around us is so beautiful. The journey is surreal, especially when we are out front blazing a trail. The dogs pull hard, their tails up, arseholes winking, only the occasional fart but a lot of shit. The sledge creaks that low groan the whole way and other than the crack of the whip, the rhythm of the dog's feet in the snow, and an occasional word from Rasmus, there are no other sounds. With the motion of the sledge, I drift off many times. I fall from the sledge, half-asleep, but keep running as I hit the snow. Rasmus turns, but simply nods at me when I clamber back onboard. I'm half embarrassed but also quite pleased I didn't end up face first in a drift.

I tried to meditate while on the sledge but found it hard, which is a sad indication of how much I've slipped back into my egoic, chattering mind. I'm constantly thinking of the film, the questions I must ask and the experiences I'm having. While this is all very useful for my job, it's preventing me from that sensation I so want to find up here: the connection with nature only found with a still mind. I get moments of it when I concentrate on my breathing, or try other simple meditation tricks, but this isn't true stillness. It will need some work but the result will be worth it. Only when I have found this natural peace will I begin to ask my hunter friends what goes on in their minds while they are moving along. I am sure that they are naturally connected but I am eager to hear more.

After many hours travelling across the ice we stop for the night at a hut at the edge of the fjord. The first thing, always, after a long day like this is to sort the dogs out, because they are everything to us, our security and our lifeline. They need feeding and separating. It's walrus on the menu again for the dogs, but I'm treated to another local speciality – raw whale skin, with a thin layer of blubber. 'It gives you energy,' says Rasmus, 'I harpooned it, then shot it, then hauled it in.' I take a bite. Imagine a fishy sandwich with a bit of rubber either side and you have the taste and texture, but it is strangely tasty. I describe this in detail for the camera. Rasmus smiles to himself, a little bemused by the whole performance. It's just fat after all.

The next job is to get some water to cook with. The sea ice is dotted with small fresh-water icebergs. As long as we have enough fuel for our cooking stoves we won't be going thirsty. I hack off some small chunks and help Rasmus prepare tonight's unusual feast – halibut curry, a first for me, for sure. The dogs will all sleep outside, perfectly warm in their thick coats, noses tucked under their tails, and warning us against the approach of a polar bear. A little while later, I nip out of the camp to have a wee and find it's broad daylight. I am, truly, in the land of the midnight sun. And how glorious it is. Of course in the winter they have the reverse, four months of the year, complete darkness. It is unbelievably beautiful, but I don't stay out for long. It's amazing how quickly a bare little appendage could cool out here. Worst case is black blisters and amputation. No thanks!

19 April: Qaanaaq Fjord

I slept well on my musk ox and reindeer skins. Who wouldn't? The little insulated wooden hut is a miracle of warmth. The hunters last night said they didn't use sleeping bags so I was worried about how I'd fare. I left my bag in my duffle but took out my trusty cashmere blanket instead, removed my duvet jacket and put on some down socks. The next thing I knew it was morning and I was sweating uncomfortably. I had somehow removed my socks and blanket in the night but I had still overheated. A layer of sweat under three layers of clothing that will remain on you for the next week isn't a

good start. But there is little I can do. My best option was to do what I did – go outside. And how welcome the cold is when you know it is just for a moment before you equalize and come back into the warm hut. It's been a slow start this morning. People have got up, melted some ice, read, made phone calls (yes, three bars reception!), filled flasks and eaten cake, biscuits, frozen fish, stale burger, spam and sardines. Arctic bliss.

I wonder whether the slow start is typical of the gentle hunter ways (not a contradiction in terms, I believe), or whether it is in some way connected to the fact that we are surrounded by freezing fog reducing visibility to about 20 metres in any direction. As our intended route is that place out in the fjord where the frozen winter ice meets the spring open waters, it doesn't surprise me that they're in no rush to go there if the visibility is bad. I haven't even asked them why yet, because I trust them implicitly and will simply go with their say so. Our intended destination is dangerous and the recent snowfall and lack of wind could even mean that there is snow lying on open water with the tiniest crust of ice, which is obviously a lethal combination and not one I'm keen on finding out for myself, especially as my sledge seems to be the fastest and usually out front. So we wait.

No sign of the crew yet. They slept in a tent placed over two sledges. They all have huge sleeping bags so will have been warm for sure, but their tent can't be as cosy as

the hut. This is a real first for me. I've had a more comfortable night than the film crew. Amazing. Maybe they're all wrapped up not wanting to break open their bags to turn the tent heater on. More likely they're up and about waiting for James, who slept next to me in the hut, to give them the word to start filming. James still hasn't been outside yet so it's probably a game of wills as to who breaches the confines of their refuge first. It's a good crew. James I know from the early days of *Tribe*, Zubin, our sound guy, did four of the six *Amazon* films and is going to do four of the five of these Arctic episodes, which I'm delighted about. Johnny the cameraman is a good find, fit and alert and easy to work with.

James has just ventured out. Just myself, Rasmus, Toku and Adolph left in the hut. They're chatting constantly so I leave my notes and join in. It's always a balance when trying to write a journal. It's a bit like filming, you're never a part of it but just observing. For most of my expedition and travelling life I never took photos or wrote diaries, preferring instead to be in the experience fully. That has all changed now that I'm paid to make television and help create books. One day I'll return to my old preferred ways, but for now I'm content as I feel it's important to share my experiences.

Rasmus is worried by some dark clouds on the horizon. This means open water, the sea ice is breaking up much earlier than expected. I ask Rasmus what he can interpret from the signs. 'We are always aware of the look of the ice, and avoid those dark patches. We are always aware of our landscape.' Rasmus's knowledge of the sea ice has been built up over a lifetime. Though I'm in expert hands, I'm going to need to stay alert. We are really venturing out into a dangerous place today, and of all the ways to go, falling into the water and under the ice is just not my favourite at all, so it doesn't take much persuading to get me to help watching the condition of the ice beneath us as we travel.

RIGHT: At camp that night, I leave the tent to go to the loo, and it's bright outside, the midnight sun!
OPPOSITE: We set up camp on the ice floe, with sledges, dogs and our mountain of camera kit. We are a small crew, with just twenty cases, but those poor dogs had to shift it all.
OVERLEAF: Low on the horizon the midnight sun sparkles above Herbert Island.

After a few hours by sledge we head into a patch of freezing fog. Quickly enveloped by a cloud of tiny ice particles, it's like we're moving through a cloud of glitter. Later we cross another long section of fjord covered in fresh deep snow. After a long day's travelling I can hear the distant sound of sea birds, and can actually smell the sea. We've reached the ice edge. It's quite one of the most magical places I've ever been, bereft of human detritus. Of course this place is connected to the rest of the world. It's not a pristine ecosystem separate from our messy southern waters, but for now it does feel clean and unspoilt. It certainly has the sensation of a natural wilderness, without humans to mess it up. No tin cans and shopping trolleys in this stretch of water. It's breathtakingly beautiful but with no sign of walrus and without a boat, my companion Paulos reminds me, we can go no further. 'If this ice was thicker we could probably walk on ice and catch walrus, but the ice here is too thin.'

The premature break up of the sea ice has caught the hunters out. It doesn't look like they'll have much chance of getting anything here. It's late. Man and dog could do with a rest so we make camp on a safe bit of land, not far from the ice edge. We're just settling down for the night when we see another team of hunters coming our way. These guys come prepared for open water. One minute you think you're the only people in the entire world and then suddenly you're overwhelmed by dogsled teams, and a boat of all things. If I'm going to have any chance of a walrus hunt, I need to get out in one of those boats. Everyone's up early the following morning. Walrus have been spotted a mile or so offshore, so the hunt is on. The hunters are happy for

THIS PAGE: The hunters gain high ground to look out over the broken sea ice for signs of walrus.

me to join one of the boats, on two conditions. First, that I wear Inuit cold-weather gear. They don't want to deal with a freezing foreigner out at sea. Secondly, that I go alone. The film crew must stay behind.

Walrus are iconic Arctic animals. They live where pack ice meets open water, diving for clams and other shellfish then hauling themselves out onto the ice to rest and sleep. They shouldn't be hard to spot. Adult walrus weigh in at more than a ton, a big prize for the hunters, well worth risking these treacherous waters. After an hour or so we make for shore again, so that we can climb up a promontory to gain a better view and scan the ice for any signs of life. But no luck so far. In between, I amuse myself shooting some film on my little camera, and playing with the ice around the boat. In some places it's like a layer of latex, semi-solid, you can wobble it, pulsating little waves out. I'm not bored, but transfixed by tiny details. The things you can do while waiting for walrus.

Before long though my idle reverie is interrupted by a shout. The stillness that we experienced at the slack of high tide is soon replaced by a surge of ice, coming our way. The walrus that were seen earlier have moved off, but that's the least of our worries. The tide is now turning, bringing massive chunks of sea ice with it, blocking our route back to the camp. It's a real maze trying to make our way through all these floes. You go into open water channels, yet soon meet a dead end. You come back out, trying to go back the way you came and the ice has closed behind you. 'If this ice

keeps coming, it will be impossible to get through,' Paulos says, 'It's all white, you can't see the open water.' All around us everything is moving and there's the constant groan of the ice, shifting in different directions as the wind is catching it.

We've just come on land again, to try to gain some altitude to look out to sea. The newest turn of events is that we're going to drag the boat across a floe, out onto the ice the other side and back into a new stretch of water, simple as that. No fuss. Finally we find a way through and make our way back to camp but none of us feel like celebrating. We're coming back empty handed, we're having to accept defeat. Didn't see a single thing all day, which was so disappointing, although in some ways it was a good day for me out on the ice and water, but for these guys sad as we really wanted to get something. The mood back at camp is subdued. Paulos tells me it's becoming much harder to hunt at this time of year. 'Nothing to catch, only birds,' he says. 'We thought it would be easy to get something here, but it's hard to predict the early break up of the ice. In the old days, spring was quite different to now, it is getting much harder to hunt.'

The one thing I'm picking up on a lot here is really how dramatically things are changing for the people who want to continue to live off the land. Once it was almost a certainty that they could get out on that ice, but now it's much warmer, the ice is softer, thinner, and shifting much earlier in the year, and that's having a real impact on these people's lives. Temperatures here have risen by more than $1°C$ in recent years, more than twice the global average, with far-reaching impacts on this frozen world, but hunters like Mads Ole are not going to give up. 'We are going to have to change our way of hunting,' he tells me in camp that evening, 'and adapt to this climate change. We can't continue to hunt in the way our forefathers did, that's obvious, but I don't think I should be sad about my future as a hunter. I just need to adapt to the world as it is now. For me hunting will always be exciting, a challenge.' The Inuit have always been adaptable, it's one of their great strengths, but they will need all of their resourcefulness to keep pace with the current warming of the Arctic.

21 APRIL: QAANAAQ FJORD

Rasmus has run out of walrus meat so the dogs will have to make do with dry biscuits. Unless we get some meat we're all going to go hungry, that's the way of it out here. The dogs need meat and we need something too. Before we head off to the seal

ABOVE LEFT: Life in camp. Toku was a real asset to us, not least for her great cooking.
ABOVE RIGHT: After greatly appreciating her fare, Rasmus brushes his teeth.
OPPOSITE: Adolph stops for a brew. The dogs, exhausted, take a moment's nap in the sunshine.

hunting grounds, however, he insists we first attend to the basics: a good cup of tea and brushing our teeth. We enjoy the simple intimacy of this shared ritual. We're looking for seal today. We have to spread out so we can observe the landscape, but it really is the proverbial needle in a haystack, there's such a flat expanse of snow. We're stopping every now and then, scanning the horizon for seals that might be out sunning themselves on the floe.

After five hours of searching, Mads Ole finally spots a ringed seal at a huge distance. I stay with the dogs while he begins to venture forward over the ice to make sure they don't chase after him. They're pining for their boss already. I hold them back with the whip until, at last, the sound of the gunshot tells us it's time to go forward together. He has taken a seal with a perfect shot right behind the eyes. Of course the last thing you'd want is for it to be injured, maimed, and for it to escape back through its hole in the ice. Looking around it would be easy to think this is a barren wasteland, but beneath our feet is a rich marine ecosystem, supporting fish, walrus and thousands of ringed seals. These are the most common marine mammals in the Arctic; they are a staple for the main predators, the polar bears and the Inuit hunters. Adolph has seen two seals on the floes close together, far ahead of us. He says I can go with him this time, as long as I camouflage myself by turning my anorak inside out. I must keep in line and stay quiet.

Before rifles arrived in the Far North Inuit hunters would have stalked seals in this way, but with a spear. It would have taken a lot of time and skill to get close enough to make a kill. Even now, it still takes almost half an hour for him to approach within firing distance. Slowly he walks, then crouches, then slides forward on the ice. Another ten minutes, he moves forward another 20 feet or so and stops to control his breathing. He gradually lies down, takes aim and fires. Like Mads Ole, he hits the seal just behind the eyes, another clean kill. This kill represents life. The only way to survive in the North is through the death of these animals. There is no other way. There is a little bit of gathering, a few berries and tubers that can be found in the summer, but otherwise all of your food comes from animals such as this. It has to be like this and to deprive people of this is to say that they must not be here. It's as simple as that. This cycle of life and death does represent the traditional way for peoples of the North.

Sadly it is the world's hunter-gatherers who are most affected by the changes to the natural world, which most of us are unaware of. Slight shifts in environmental conditions can have dramatic effects on animals and their habits, which in turn can have a huge effect on the success of the hunt. Only when I am out on the ice, cold but alive and alert, can I get the faintest glimpse of what life for the Inuit of Greenland in days past must have been like. In Africa or in the jungle, if a hunter didn't catch his meat he could collect berries or fruit or tubers; he may go hungry but not cold. Here animals provide food, clothing, shelter and the means to heat the shelter. Meat and blubber, bones, skin and antler is everything for life.

While I was with Adolph, Rasmus got a seal of his own. We head off to look for a place to camp and after an hour or so, stop by a glacial iceberg for fresh water. As soon as the tents are up, Adolph starts to butcher his seal. He takes care not to rip the skin, which is used to make gloves and boots. 'We use every part of it,' he explains,

wielding his short knife with a surgeon's precision. 'It's only the *sungaq* (gall-bladder) that we don't need.' The skin will be used for clothing for the family, or be given away or sold if it's a nice pelt and they have no need for it. Of course all the meat and blubber will be eaten, both by the family and dogs. If it's been freshly cut soon after the kill on the ice, many hunters will eat the liver. And then the bits that the humans might not want – the flippers, the tail – the dogs eat without a second's thought. The Inuit used to be called Eskimos, 'eaters of raw meat' by the Cree tribe in northern Canada. In the days before kerosene, meat would only be cooked up here if absolutely necessary and raw seal remains popular today.

Chewy, steamy, seal stomach skin with liver is my lunch and Adolph cuts me a piece straight from the carcass. So tender, it melts, almost vanishes in my mouth. It's one of the best things I've ever tasted. I ask for a second helping but Adolph offers me something even more exotic: a freshly squeezed seal eyeball. This is right up there on the list of the weirdest things I've ever eaten and the thought of gulping it down is horrendous. The camera rolls, I close my eyes and tuck in. In actual fact, it tasted like a pretty bland jelly but I won't be doing it again, ever. When we've eaten our fill it's the dogs' turn, who deserve it far more than we do, having pulled us non-stop for about 60 kilometres. The dogs have done all of that work – hard work – and they deserve every bit of this. We settle in camp for the night.

Though climate change is making things unpredictable out on the ice, Rasmus is more worried about imposed limits on the animals he can kill. New quotas have been recently introduced after pressure from outsiders, particularly animal rights campaigners. 'We are hunters,' he says, 'but we don't wipe out the animals. We just get a few. We are friendlier to the environment than polluting countries. They don't understand us. They've limited us too much and I don't like it.' It's time to head back to Qaanaaq. We didn't get any big animals but at least we're not going back empty handed. There are so few traditional hunters left in Greenland, they are much more endangered than the animals they are hunting. Though I understand the need for controls, it would be a tragedy if the Inuit were forced to give up this way of life and their connection with the Arctic environment was broken.

24 APRIL: QAANAAQ

After a long day travelling across the ice, we finally pull in to town. Life out on the sea ice felt timeless and ancient, but town is very different. It was Saturday evening when we got back and so we all went straight to the community hall where Mads Ole was due to play lead guitar for a room full of mixed aged ravers – a kind of heavy rock meets Scandinavian pop. He truly is a *modern* hunter. Everyone seems to know his every word and they dance, slapping and spinning through the air. Before long though, most of the crew head for the pub.

THIS PAGE: Progress is slow and challenging as we pick our way through the chaotic tumble of broken ice.

Rasmus takes me to the supermarket to stock up on supplies for his next hunting trip. At first sight, with the same old aisles and grim artificial lighting, you really could be anywhere in the world. I say that, but there are bullets racked up next to the cigarettes, and sausages and steaks sharing space in the freezer cabinets with seal meat. Powdered milk in a can will set you back £12, vegetables are flown in from Europe and North America. An apple costs £1. These things are expensive, but it's no real shock. If you want it, that's the way of it. But, surprisingly, the expense of these foods is nothing compared to the traditional meat bought in this way – a small chunk of narwhal is about £20. This is good in one respect: if a hunter is successful he might be able to make a small bit of money, but he kills just a few narwhal a year, so it's impossible to earn a living in the modern sense or save any significant money because of the restrictions. I worry when I learn about some hunting for money here. Once subsistence becomes commercial it is such a slippery slope. Rasmus needs to earn cash to live in town, but he's only allowed to hunt enough to feed his family.

It's a fragile, subsistence way of life, hand to mouth, with little to spare. The family can only afford to shop here because of the money that Rasmus's wife Malia brings in from her job as a nursery school teacher. Our grocery bill this time comes in at over £160 for just a few essential items, including the bullets. Clearly it's not an easy existence. 'I would be better paid if I had a job. Being a hunter it is very expensive to live and as a worker, you may have a better life.' It's not just the supermarket that's costly.

Rasmus and Malia need to pay for their heating and electricity. The high price of living is forcing more and more hunters to look for modern work. Many men have left their families, travelling to southern Greenland to find jobs, but if a hunter is lucky out on the ice he can still just about get by. The most renowned narwhal hunter in Qaanaaq is now a cleaner in an old peoples' home.

25 APRIL: QAANAAQ

It's Sunday morning and there's a carnival atmosphere as everyone gathers on the sea ice. I thought I'd seen the end of dogs and sledges, but I was very much mistaken, because today the whole village is having a race. Every spring the hunters in Qaanaaq compete against each other and though it's only for fun there's a real tension in the air. I've been roped in, but luckily I'm back with my good friend Rasmus. Unburdened by fuel, food and equipment, the sledges race off at an almighty pace. It's 35 kilometres of gnashing and whip-cracking fun. Bloody cold too. No polar bear trousers, and my top-of-the-range hill-walking boots were about as useful as brogues on Ben Nevis when it came to insulation. Among the thirty or so sledges in the race, we were well positioned by the half way mark, with just two turns on the course out across the bay. I gave a piece to camera, commenting with gusto as we emerged at the corner, breaking clear from a mass of legs and runners. I put on an animated show, like a sports commentator, waffling to camera about a neck-and-neck race, and then got

frustrated at myself, realizing that it was more acceptable to get excited over this than much of the deeper issues we've encountered so far. Our addiction to sport is a funny thing. I'm glad I managed to wean myself off it.

Victorious, the winning musher is raised aloft sitting on his sledge and carried back into town. He shares news of his success with his friends, texting them on his mobile phone. Having spent time on the ice with the hunters, perhaps looking tightly at the past, it's great to see the community out together and interesting to see quite how modern the village has become. Everyone here has a mobile phone and most have an email address. Only a few decades ago the majority of Greenlanders were living in stone dwellings with turf roofs in small isolated villages, hunting and fishing. Today, nearly all have moved into towns like Qaanaaq, to live modern, settled lives.

Moments after the race has finished, word spreads through the village that a hunter has shot a polar bear, some 40 kilometres out on the sea ice. A few hours later, he returns from the hunt and by the time I arrive a large crowd has gathered to meet him. Though the bear is a familiar sight, it's still an honoured kill and everyone is excited to see it. The skin and joints are already in buckets ready to be loaded and taken home. The local police car offers its services to ferry the meat back to his house. As the crowd disperses, I ask the hunter about his prize. 'Those parts will be eaten by humans, some of it will be for my youngest son's birthday. It tastes very, very good.' Each year a local hunter is only allowed to kill a single polar bear. I know the quotas are causing a lot of resentment, but it's good that endangered species are given some protection. He agreed that there were more bears in the area now because the thinning of the ice was forcing them south. He wasn't convinced that numbers were dwindling but would be happy to collaborate with the scientists and conservationists

RIGHT: A hunter returns with a prize kill – a polar bear. Butchered out on the ice, the meat will feed his family and friends for many weeks. By the time I arrive, just the skin remains. I struggle to find the right words when I speak my piece for the camera.

to discover the facts. He expressed how important the fur was for their clothing. The eating is good and the kudos high.

I find it hard to sum up for the camera what I feel about the shooting of a polar bear. I know it's really important for them. I've just been wearing polar bear trousers all of last week and I understand the reasons why, culturally, they still hunt the bear. Yes, I do find it hard to stand here, holding the skin of this polar bear and talking to our camera, as I'd rather see it still alive, but I'd be a hypocrite to speak out against the hunt. I'm not out there, day by day, in the freezing cold trying to feed my family, trying to make a life from hunting. But as these people accept more modern conveniences from outside they may have to deal with outside opinion too.

The rapid change here has left many people feeling disorientated, overwhelmed and dislocated. The country has the highest suicide rate in the world. Alcoholism, child abuse and domestic violence plague many communities. It's time to leave the high Arctic and journey south. I want to find out more about this recent modernization and the challenges and opportunities it has created. At the airport in Qaanaaq, Rasmus and Malia come to see me off. I ask him a final question. What does the future hold? 'I have thought about it,' he tells me, 'but I'm not sure if I can continue as a hunter. The future is so uncertain for a hunter. I don't want to but maybe it would be better if I got a job.'

ABOVE: Fishing boats lie idle on the frozen shore until the ice retreats later in the summer.
OVERLEAF: A polar bear leaps across melting ice along Sabinebukta Bay, Irminger Point, Svalbard.

THE POLAR BEAR Of all the international concern about the Arctic, it is the survival of polar bears that usually captures most attention. Born in dens in remote snowdrifts nestled along coastlines from Greenland, Arctic Canada, Svalbard to Alaska, polar bears spend most of their lives roaming the floating ice on the sea in search of seals. *Ursus maritimus* is its scientific name, literally the 'sea bear'. Here, the Inuit know the bear as *nanoq*, the 'great wanderer'.

For past explorers, the bear was once an enemy to be vanquished, a prize to be hunted above all others. Now the polar bear is a victim, a symbol of what we stand to lose in the North, emblematic of the whole Arctic and the health of its ecology. Contaminants, pollution and climate change have, in recent years, placed polar bear populations in danger. Current estimates suggest there are 20,000 bears surviving in the wild. This is predicted to decrease by more than 30 per cent within three generations. If these estimates are accurate, some US surveys declare that two-thirds of the world's polar bears will disappear by 2050. By 2080, they would disappear from Greenland entirely, with dwindling populations along the Russian coast and scattered Arctic islands.

In 2008, the USA listed the polar bear under the Endangered Species Act and banned all importing of polar bear skins. Some 500–900 bears are still hunted each year, mainly by Inuit subsistence hunters, who honour the bear, still central to their cosmological beliefs, and depend upon it to provide them with skins and meat. Traditionally, consuming food from these mammals is a fundamental part of social identity and cultural wellbeing, an important part of both physical and spiritual nourishment. It is the chang-ing nature of the sea ice that poses the greatest threat to these majestic predators, and traditions may be forced to change in line with this.

In a recent article, *Guardian* newspaper columnist George Monbiot urged his readers to 'forget the sodding bears, this is about all of us'. Writing about the impacts of climate change, it is important to realize that they are hitting closer to home than most people imagine. We are all intimately connected to the Arctic. A frozen Arctic plays a central role in regulating the Earth's climate, with critical feedbacks affecting the global system, from altering ocean circulation to increased emissions of greenhouse gases from thawing permafrost soils. The rapidly shrinking

amount of reflective ice also plays a significant part, and we may be pushed beyond a tipping point into serious trouble.

A recent WWF report, considering the fate of the increasingly melting ice sheets of Greenland and Antarctica, projected that sea levels will very plausibly rise by more than one metre by 2100, largely due to increased mass loss from the ice sheets. This is more than twice the amount scientists projected in 2007. In this new scenario, a quarter of the world's population could be affected by a rise of this magnitude, with flooding, shoreline erosion and saltwater intrusion into surface waters and farmland. Melting in the Arctic is a global problem.

OPPOSITE I join a Swiss climbing team, working to clear the cliff face for a new mine entrance high above the Uummannaq Fjord. At bottom left, the small terminus for a new cable car has just been finished. It's great working up here in the sunshine, but I dread to think what it must be like at minus 40°.

The Inuit are slowly, inevitably, losing their traditions, like ice melting away. Some are trying hard to retain their links to the past, to the land of their ancestors. Others are looking forward into the future, eager to embrace the changes. I hope that Rasmus and a few others are able to continue hunting up here in Qaanaaq, maintaining their intimate connection with this incredible landscape.

28 APRIL: MAAMORILIK

With every degree of latitude I fly south, the temperature rises, with relative changes on the freezing sea. We haven't been flying long but already there are signs of the ice pack breaking up, and ahead of me I can see that it's really quite dramatic. I'm flying halfway down Greenland's west coast to an area called Disko Bay. This region is rich in oil, metal ores and gemstones. These fjords and mountains are fast becoming a new resource frontier. The Greenland government hope the wealth and jobs created here will seal the country's transformation into a modern economy. Qaanaaq has given me a glimpse of Greenland's past, now I want to look into its future.

I'm heading out into the wilderness again, but this time I have a very different guide. Tim Daffern is an Australian and he's a mining entrepreneur. Greenland is warming so fast, the vast ice sheet that covers its interior is melting at an unprecedented rate, exposing new land and new riches. 'Fundamentally,' he tells me, as we gaze out from the windows of his helicopter, 'the area over which we are flying now, if you went back ten years ago, and certainly twenty-five or thirty years ago, we'd be flying over solid ice. The simple fact is the ice has now gone. What this allows us to do is to expand our geological exploration work. When you've got eighty or even a hundred metres of ice there was no way you can see the rock.' Just five years ago, while hiking on these rocks, Tim discovered a billion-dollar deposit of zinc and lead that had previously been covered by a glacier.

A zinc seam was first discovered at the 'Black Angel' cliff in the 1960s and exploited in the following decade as one of the richest zinc seams ever found. The tunnel and shafts extended hundreds of kilometres into the landscape. The first mine was environmentally very damaging and the waste lead and other metals and pollutants were poured straight into the sea. The mine has been closed for almost twenty years but because of the recent resurgence in zinc prices, and improved technology, which gives access to new areas, it has become commercially viable once again. Added to that you have a retreating ice shelf and glaciers, such as those that Tim described, which are revealing new seams previously invisible to even seismic technology.

The new entrance to the mine is 600 metres above sea level and access is tricky to say the least. After a helicopter flight, and a vertical descent down ladders clinging to the cliff face, we reach the entrance to the mine. The zinc deposit is hundreds of metres inside the mountain; high explosives have replaced picks and shovels in modern

BELOW: The mine is about 5 kilometres long and is located deep inside the Black Angel mountain. The entrance is high on the cliff face, about 600 metres above the waters of the fjord. Despite the exhilaration of the blast, I feel strange about the way the Earth is being raided here.

OPPOSITE: A joyful view at the end of a hard day. In the summer, this fjord is full of whales.

OVERLEAF: Meltwater from an iceberg that has broken away from the Ilulissat Kangerlus- suaq Glacier cascades into the sea in Disko Bay.

mining. Zinc doesn't rust, so it's used in the construction industry to coat steel. There's a huge global demand for it, particularly within the booming economies of India and China. Tim points out a large lump of galena, the natural mineral form of lead sulphide, the most important lead ore. 'In today's terms,' he explains, standing in the mine shaft, his face lit by our camera, 'the amount of metal in this pillar deposit in front of us is about one and a half million dollars. There are about a thousand of them in this mine. Our estimate is in excess of a billion dollars worth of metal here in this mountain.'

I ask if this potential fortune carries with it certain responsibilities? 'Sure,' he says, 'we have to be aware of the environmental consequences. One of the things we're very careful to make sure of is that all of our processing is here underground, so we have no waste – liquid or solid – that leaves this mine. All that comes out is concen- trated metal, secured in bags inside special steel boxes and then carried down across the fjord.' I am reassured by his talk, but wonder if the development will measure up to this clean PR version when it's actually finished? I really want to believe him and in the occasional off-camera moment I break through the polished chat to a human and find that I do believe him. But sadly, like so many of us, he is just a small cog in a much larger machine, one that can supersede his desire to do the right thing. In my opinion money is the biggest voice in this world.

This is Tim's project and he's proud of it. The aim is to be 100 per cent toxin free, an environmentally neutral mine, which has low impact on the natural surroundings but which has a positive impact on the local population. In a nutshell, I thought that Tim's philosophy was good. Somehow he had managed to hold back the usual cred- itors and demands for a quick buck and higher profits, and designed a mine that should work over a long time period and nurture the locals into a possible future in

similar projects. With fish stocks depleting in this area, the Greenlanders are increasingly desirous of a major new income and this could be it. In my experience big industry alongside indigenous peoples is almost always catastrophic. The locals have been drawn into a new cash economy which persuades them to forget their old ways for the new mine or mill, then leaves them high and dry when it goes.

Tim's desire to make this a long-term prospect should counter this issue if done correctly. The idea to do all of the chemical processing inside the existing mine will also go some way to help control the environmental impact. But with the question of money though, the same old story remains. Most of the profits will leave Greenland. Press friendly measures like local football teams, improved schooling and healthcare provision are but a drop in the ocean compared to the real money being made here. But that is the global economic system and Tim can't be held accountable for that. He is operating within the system and is doing as well as he can bearing in mind the finances at play. The backers that have footed the bill and taken the risk will only let him go so far. I wish him well but wish that life was different.

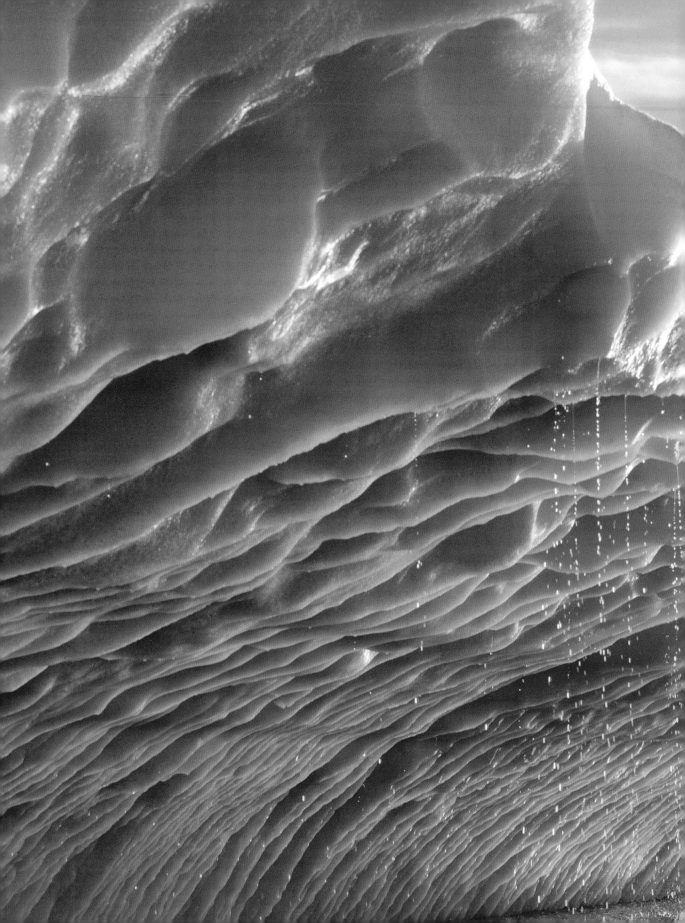

THE RICHES OF GREENLAND

Greenland has been in the international spotlight since the inauguration of Self-Government; an Act passed on its national day on 21 June 2009. The Act allows for the gradual, further transfer of powers and responsibilities from Denmark to Greenland, in various domestic areas such as the administration of justice, the establishment of police and healthcare provision. Most importantly, the Act provides for Greenland's own administration of the control and use of mineral and oil resources, so that any public revenues from mineral and oil activities in the future belong to Greenland. Having fought for many years, the Greenlandic Inuit language Kalaallisut is also now recognized as the official language of the country.

Denmark has promised to allow the islanders full sovereignty if they can match the subsidies currently received, which if oil is found will not take long at all, depending on the rate at with which they exploit it. Various political parties within the country stress different methods and speeds for separating with Denmark but most voices consider them at least a part of their future. In order to establish the necessary financial foundation to supplement their fishing industry, and limited land-based activities such as tourism and sheep farming, Greenlanders are currently debating and preparing to embark on a series of major development projects.

Unsurprisingly most of these focus on resources, in particular minerals and petroleum. There is potential for gold, base metals, even diamonds. The likelihood of 'rare earth elements' found in ore deposits is one interesting avenue, perfectly timed to meet the insatiable demand for these valuable minerals, used extensively in electronics, batteries, high magnets and mobile phones. China currently controls amost 90 per cent of the world's rare earth deposits and processing. International mining companies are interested in getting a foothold here.

Much of the land is still unexplored. Greenland has the right to a resource base and the right for development to be carried out to the highest standards, utilizing the best available technology and minimizing the environmental risks. The balance in the speed of any oil and mineral extraction will depend on which domestic party forges the way and how they manage it.

ABOVE: Enjoying the sunshine on Uummannaq Fjord, I'm given a snazzy new pair of glasses based on an old Inuit snow-goggle design.
OPPOSITE AND FOLLOWING PAGES: The fjord is now free of the majority of the winter ice, but beautiful bergs remain. When icebergs tip over, they can easily flood a small boat like this. With even larger bergs, the waves can overwhelm the boat.

I want to get a sense of the challenges facing miners in Greenland. Tim's first task is getting a cable car up to the tunnel entrance. For that he needs specialists, and they don't come more specialized than this Swiss climbing and blasting crew. I spend the afternoon with Niels, Fritz, and the rest of their mountain team. What a great bunch of guys. I tried chatting to them last night when we sat together at dinner after their twelve-hour shift but didn't get much response. Heads down, dusty, beards matted, and with forearms like my calves. They're an enigmatic bunch. We have only a little time for them on film, but they give me a quick insight into working life here. This group of seven are all from valleys of German-speaking Switzerland and they're naturals at dangling from ropes in cold and extreme weather. They came here well prepared to be tying fiddly knots in temperatures below minus 40°C, sometimes a long way beneath that temperature. They are calm, no words of bravado or macho showing off. They just exuded real toughness of the type I truly admire and rarely see at home.

I love them and after showing that I could hang upside down on a rope and not cry too much they warmed to me just a little. They are mostly here on stints of five or six months with the very occasional day off at the local village for a rest. Unlike most of the long-term contractors here, once the cable car and escape ladders and safety nets are in place, their work will be done and these boys will take their cash and go their separate ways. Some will go on holiday, some on expeditions, some back home to rest up awhile. They have spent the last year clearing the rock face of loose debris. The last job of the day is typical: we pack a measured section of rock with dynamite and stand well back, retreating inside the mountain shaft. I'm given the job of pressing the switch to blow the lot. I get a moment's thrill at the blast but then the whole next day feel weird about it. Something isn't quite right. Is this respecting the landscape?

In little more than another year, once this area has been cleared, the cable car will be installed and mining will begin. Though most of the set-up is being done by outsiders, there are a few local men here doing unskilled jobs. I join some for lunch and ask them how this compares with traditional work. 'I prefer working here rather than hunting or fishing,' one says, 'both of those rely on the weather, too much uncertainty. When I changed from being a fisherman to working in the mine I had steady money coming in which helped pay my bills, like the telephone and rent, things, you know, things that we used not to have to find money for. Other people don't have the opportunity to do work like this at the moment, but I hope a lot of people will come and work in the mines.' When the mine is fully operational it will employ 120 local people, with many more working in support industries. Six more mines are about to open in Greenland, creating thousands of jobs. The government has got its eye fixed firmly on resource development.

4 MAY: UUMMANNAQ

The rapid transition to a modern, industrial society has a downside. I've come to the nearby town of Uummannaq. It's a typical Greenlandic settlement, picturesque but sadly beset by social problems. I meet with orphaned and abused children, the victims of Greenland's frenetic pace of change. Some of their stories are unimaginable. One girl was very nearly killed by her drunken mother, another recently attempted suicide. Social campaigner Ole Jørgen Hammeken and his wife Anne run an innovative children's home here. He believes the key to the children's future lies with the last of Uummannaq's hunters. 'The old way of life that the hunters grew up with,' he tells me one afternoon, 'is something the children can experience in safety with us. Here is such a place where they can learn the importance of being calm and a more relaxed way of life. At the same time, they can experience what it is like to be close to nature and understand the character of the hunter.'

I join Ole and Anne on a trip to an abandoned village, out on an island in the bay. The island was where it all began to make sense. Ole Jørgen and his team of hunters were all hanging out while the kids played, but on occasion you saw them interact and always it was with mutual respect. This was a new thing for the hunters. Some of them were unsure of what to make of the kids from broken homes in the capital Nuuk who were frustrated at the solitude of Uummannaq. One method often used for new arrivals was to send them to the island we were visiting. It sounds ominous but seemed to work very well. Here the children's mobile phones would soon run out of battery and before long they'd be desperate with boredom. After some time – they can all spend up to three months on the island during the summer – they would have to find entertainment among themselves, and with nature. Reading and writing came later when the child requested it, which they nearly always did. But first was therapy for the mind, which the natural world can offer and who better to be the conduit for that world than the hunters.

Of course, many kids at first would simply play with each other but there were also hunting and fishing exercises led by the hunters. This was interesting too because the hunters have a way about them which is very different to the average mind of the city. Theirs is a Zen-like approach to life, based on quietening the constant chatter of the mind and being present in the moment, being aware. The kids could tap into this, becoming more relaxed, more imaginative, finding a little of themselves. These were great lessons to be shared.

Ole Jørgen and some of the elders take them out on hunting trips, sometimes for weeks at a time. 'I really believe that these hunters can teach the children things that will help them in later life. Greenland is going through so many changes, so it's important to experience being close to nature. If the hunter's connection to the natural world disappears then it would be a great loss for our people. We would lose our identity.'

I had fun with the kids, Jane and Frankie in particular. They were wonderful children but I was aware that I had to be careful. On other occasions, in other parts of the world, I could be tactile with some kids, offering to walk with hands held or place an elbow on a shoulder. Here they evidently needed trust first and I didn't earn that in my short visit. Their tortured pasts make it particularly hard for them to feel close to strangers, no matter how well meaning they might be. Staying with Ole Jørgen and Anne in their Arctic home was lovely. Their house was full of drums, skulls, tusks and carvings. It was a veritable museum; lamp-stands made of elegant narwhal tusks, every shelf littered with amulets, model kayaks, local stones. The food was fantastic and the hospitality warm. We chatted endlessly about Greenland and indigenous peoples everywhere. Anne shared stories of the Faroe Islands and her family's fishing business, and her trips to Ibiza my home island to fetch salt. Ole Jørgen was just back from Paris and the premiere of a film he'd just starred in, *On Thin Ice*, describing the story of the orphanage and the children's relationship with the hunters. I think it was a magnificent film and highlighted beautifully some of the issues facing modern Greenland, its social problems and its cultural past. It was made by a French independent company and I wished it well.

For forty years the government has been forcing people to move from scattered hunting and fishing settlements into towns like Uummannaq. The price for this progress is the social turmoil that dogs almost all Greenlandic communities. It was really evident to me when I was with the people of Qaanaaq hunting, we were out on the sledges for seven days, and most of that time we were sat in stillness, experiencing the serenity of the surroundings. The hunters really are particularly unique beings, connected to the landscape, in a tangible way I believe, and that's what they are trying to pass on here to these children. That's also what many cultures are losing today, that connection with the landscape, that spiritual, fundamental link to nature. In a small, but meaningful way I think, this is an attempt to try and regain that. I really support what they are trying to do here. This orphanage's methods are proving successful and others are now trying to include similar ideas.

It's time for me to leave Greenland and to begin the next leg of my Arctic journey. Since the first hunters arrived here thousands of years ago, people had to adapt to survive. Today, they are suffering greatly from a rapid shift in lifestyle and identity and this troubled transition has left many hiding in the bottle, looking for comfort in drugs and alcohol. Sadly it will be the children of this generation who will suffer most, but there are some who understand the issues and are dong what they can to help them on their path to recovery. This is one positive story in a time of tremendous uncertainty. Climate change may be altering the landscape, but the seismic shifts in culture are much more challenging. The Inuit of Greenland will need all the resourcefulness of their ancestors to find their place in the Arctic of the twenty-first century.

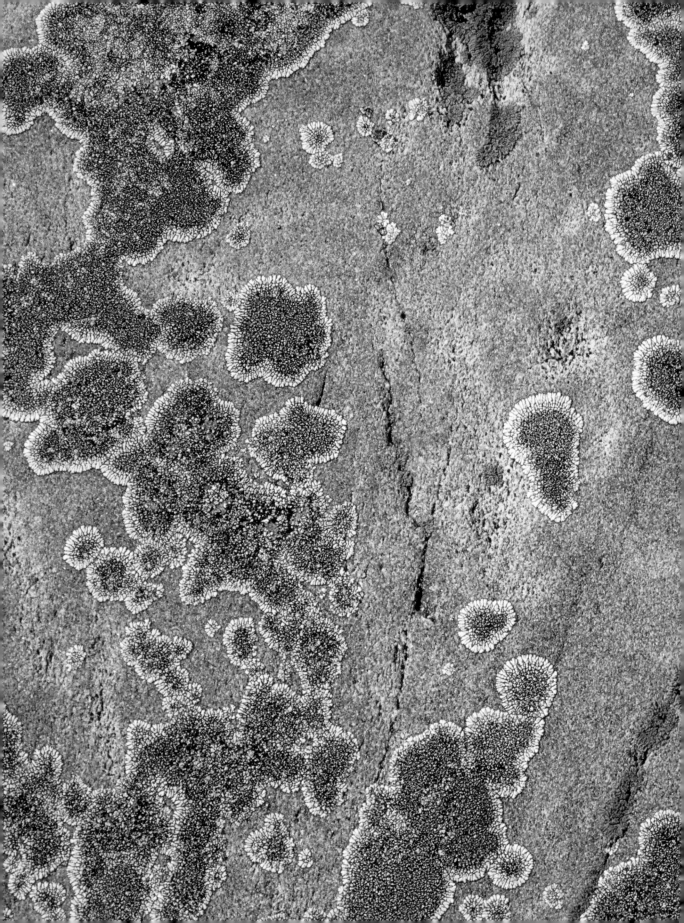

CANADA

Canada
FEAR IN THE FOREST

'You know, the caribou can't talk for themselves, so we have to talk for them. Even though we kill them, and we eat them, they provide us, our families, with life, our way of life.'

It's early spring. Across the whole of the Arctic the snow is starting to melt and the caribou herds are on the move. I've come to Canada to visit two tribes living either side of the Arctic Circle. The Gwitchin are a traditional hunting people that have a special relationship with the caribou stretching back thousands of years. I go on a hunt with these caribou people and join in a celebration of their ancient way of life. To the south of the Arctic Circle I encounter a very different tribe, living in the middle of the biggest industrial site in the world. I meet the ordinary men and women working to feed their families. They've made a pact with the oil industry, but they've paid a heavy price. The quest for oil is opening up new frontiers. How are the indigenous people of the Arctic dealing with the arrival of the modern world? And what sacrifices will have to be made in the name of progress?

10 MAY: OLD CROW

I've travelled to the tiny, remote village of Old Crow, about 130 kilometres north of the Arctic Circle in the North Yukon region close to the Alaskan border. It's home to the Vuntut Gwitchin people, who share an ancient spiritual connection with the caribou. In the Gwitchin creation story, the caribou and the Gwitchin made an agreement that they would retain a part of each other's heart, so their fates are entwined together for eternity. Like their ancestors, the people of Old Crow are sub-sistence hunters and are dependant on the caribou for their year-round supply of food. They're among the most traditional indigenous people in the whole of Canada, and despite some modern trappings, their way of life has remained essentially unchanged for thousands of years.

Somewhere out there is a herd of 130,000 caribou heading north on its annual migration and for the people in the community of Old Crow it's one of the most important times of the year. I'm joining Stephen Frost and his family on their tradi-tional spring hunt. We're with Stephen's daughter Margaret and their neighbour Robert, gearing up for a week-long hunting trip to Stephen's cabin downriver. Stephen has a foot in two worlds. His father was a white Mountie, his mother was Gwitchin, and he grew up in the wilderness learning the ways of his mother's people, with a touch of his father's farming knowhow. Traditionally the whole tribe would go out hunting caribou together, but now the Gwitchin hunt in small family groups with rifles, speedboats and shotguns.

The spring melting of the river signals the arrival of the caribou. This year the seasonal temperature has been eight degrees warmer than usual and the break-up of the river has arrived two weeks early. Loose bergs lie scattered along the river bank, like the debris of some great natural battlefield. It's a disarming sight, and apparently unusual for so early in the season. 'The caribou are tough, they'll always find a way to cross the river somehow. But, this is not a normal break up,' Stephen tells me. 'We had a lot of warm weather, the break up came early.' His explanation is interrupted as we move round the river bend, and discover some caribou in the shallows, tentatively testing the water, waiting to cross. Stephen spots them first.

There's about twenty head here, in this little outlying group of the main Porcu-pine Herd, so named after this great river we are travelling along. We don't shoot these caribou as they're all females and should be pregnant at this time of year. The herd is decreasing in number each year, so the Gwitchin now only hunt the males. Each spring the caribou migrate 500 kilometres from the Yukon territories across the Por-cupine River to their calving grounds across the border in Alaska's Arctic National Wildlife Refuge. The caribou are constantly on the move, travelling up to 50 kilo-metres a day in small groups and always on the lookout for predators. To reach their calving grounds they must run a gauntlet of bears, wolves and, of course, the Gwitchin, among other peoples. Stephen's ancestors established their territory in this region thousands of years ago, as it is right in the path of the caribou and is rich in wildfowl and other animals for hunting at other times of year.

As we made our way aong the river I saw my first ever beaver in the wild, really beautiful just swimming alongside us, and then the boat behind took a shot, which of course is why we are out here – I'm a guest on this hunt. I'd forgotten, in some sort

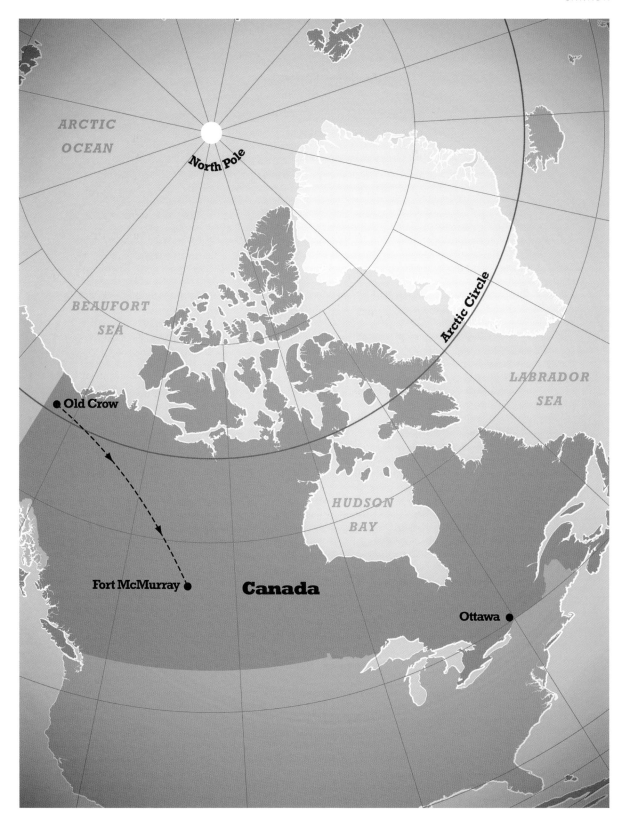

ARCTIC
OCEAN

North Pole

Arctic Circle

BEAUFORT
SEA

LABRADOR
SEA

● Old Crow

HUDSON

BAY

Fort McMurray ●

Canada

Ottawa ●

of romantic moment, that hunting is what we were here for. The first shot missed but soon the beaver was taken. Our supper is secure.

Finally we arrive at Stephen's cabin, Bluefish Lodge. Once we're settled in, it's time to skin the beaver. 'I cut all four feet off first,' Stephen describes, brandishing his knife with veteran precision. 'Lots of people don't really know why the meat's important to us, what it means to us to hunt and cook up a beaver. It's a significant thing.' Now it's my turn with the knife and I've got to be very careful not to tear it, or to hack at the joints and snap the small bones, or I'm in big trouble. Stephen jokes with me, 'It's not the end of the world if you cut the skin, but it's close to for you...' For our first evening in camp, it's beaver stew on the menu. 'Right,' he says with a smile, 'enough of this fancy stuff, let's boil the living Jesus out of it!'

Old Crow is over 400 kilometres from the nearest major settlement, and this camp is a further two hours by boat, deeper into the wilderness. The camp itself is a dream, a mix of old and new. The log cabin is surrounded by heavy-duty, electric-wire fencing to keep the bears out. There's a polite notice on the door asking them to stay away. The place is littered with stuff but it's all totally serviceable and clean in an outdoorsy sort of way. Peter, a huge bear of a man, has his hunting cabin right next door, his wife Marjory has come to join us too, and we spend the evening sharing stories around the fire. Despite the fact I'm here with a film crew, and Stephen and his family are close by, there is a real sense of solitude. It is only recently that I have realized the importance of being happy with one's own company, especially in the outdoors. It's something much misunderstood by us when we're in the city. The vistas here are massive, the skies seem to go on forever. I feel a joyous sense of calm and wellbeing. Nature herself feels immediate and alive in me and all around us.

15 May: Bluefish Camp

The next morning, after a breakfast of pancakes and bacon, I head out with Robert and Stephen's son Peter, who's just joined us, on the lookout for caribou. After some time we chug alongside the mud bank, arriving at a point where the river narrows and then snakes off into the forest. We climb a nearby hill to make better sense of this bewildering, vast terrain. This hill has served as a lookout for the Gwitchin people for millennia, watching for the caribou herd on their annual passage north. However, the caribou are highly sensitive to changes in the environment, and the gradual warming of the Arctic may be affecting this ancient pattern of migration.

BELOW LEFT: My host is hunter and woodsman, Stephen Frost.
BELOW RIGHT: A skinned caribou head slowly cooks over the fire.
OVERLEAF: Large sections of the Porcupine River are unusually ice free for the time of year.

The forest stretches out before us and we scan the land with our binoculars for any sign of movement. I can't see anything and my new friends are disheartened. 'There's normally hundreds in this spot,' Robert explains disappointedly, 'they usually are lying around on the ice where it's nice and cool.' But there is no ice on the river now. 'Everything is changing, the land is sending us a message. Even the river is behaving differently, the ice goes out earlier, at other times appears or breaks apart when we least expect it.' Peter agrees. 'All our people have been brought up on the caribou. I'm not going to change, but we will have to when the caribou stop coming here. Our traditional way of living is disappearing like the ice.'

We decide to change tactics. Robert and Peter are convinced the caribou have passed through this land early, and that if we head yet further upriver, we may just catch up with some of the stragglers. A few hours later, our strategy pays off. We glimpse a small group swimming across the river, only their heads visible above the swollen waters. But just as the caribou are about to leave the water, our boat gets stuck on a gravel bank in the riverbed. Some bulls turn, as if to head back from where they came, and it gives our hunters time for a second chance. They make no mistakes this time, and within a minute or two they have three clean kills. Single shots through the neck, almost instant death. Peter took one, standing up as no one steered the boat. The rest of the caribou wheel round and lollop for the safety of the forest.

With the gun practically still smoking, Peter and Robert quickly get to work gutting the three kills on shore. It seems to me a lot to get in one moment, but all of the meat will be dried and will last the family for some time. The caribou are decapitated where they lie. I thought this butchery a little dramatic until I saw the reason why. A little sack of bot fly larvae, alien grubs in a pod, were pulsating at the back of the animals' throats. Bot flies deposit live larvae in the nostrils of the caribou. From there the larvae move through the nasal passages into the throat. Had the heads been left on, the larvae would have left the pod and crawled deeper into the head and neck necessitating a lot of cleaning. I was then shown the other parasites that plague these poor animals, the warble fly, which lays eggs in the thick fur on their legs and bellies. When the larvae hatch they burrow into the caribou, under its skin, making their way up the legs and onto their backs, where they grow for over a year or so, close to the spine.

They are all infested like this and some even carry up to 2,000 of them. The larvae then munch little exit holes in the skin, crawl out and drop to the ground to pupate and develop into adult flies. I said to the camera it was the most disgusting thing I've ever seen and I wasn't exaggerating. I even felt a little funny later that night going to sleep which is something that has never happened to me before. I feel genuinely sorry for the caribou. In the summer you can see them shaking their heads violently, stamping their feet and galloping wildly over the tundra, for no apparent reason. They are desperately trying to find a moment's peace from these horrible little creatures.

OPPOSITE: My hunting companions, Robert and Peter, are on the lookout for caribou. A pair have just swum across the river and climb to safety up the river bank.

OPPOSITE : Another adult male was not so lucky. Stephen shows me the correct way to carefully skin the animal. I had never seen such clean butchery as this. All the meat will be eaten and we return to camp to smoke it.
OVERLEAF : A caribou herd cross the river during their annual migration across the Utukok Uplands, Alaska.

Standing on the shore, knife in hand, there isn't really time to pause for thought. The meat and edible organs are cleanly cut and put aside, and the rest is left for the scavengers. I have no bloodlust and I am a bit wary of having a reputation in my films for always following hunts. Television always seems to need a kill and having missed the walrus in Greenland – a combination of thinning ice and just bad planning – it is a relief that we've managed to capture an important part of life here on camera. Stephen's son Peter says his peoples' fate is closely tied to the caribou, and they never kill too many out of respect for the animals. 'I only take what I need. A lot of times, when we see them, we might not shoot. If my family doesn't need meat then I won't take any. I like seeing the caribou coming through the country here, it makes our land alive.'

We set off downriver back towards Stephen's camp, but a few minutes into our journey we come across a mass of floating ice. The Crow River is breaking up and charging down into the Porcupine, so we have to get to the bank quicky to avoid smashing up the boat. Robert and Peter are looking pretty worried as they watch thousands of tons of ice flowing past. And it turns out we could be here for some time, unless we make a dash for it through the churning stream. I hope we run the gauntlet, but it's easy for me to say that – it's not my boat...

After more discussions we decide to go for it, to see if we can get ahead of the ice. Robert is in control, and he is happy to have moved on. 'Beautiful and dangerous, that's the way it always is. That's what life is like when you are living on the edge,' he jokes to reassure himself, as small bergs claw their way along the sides of our metal hull. It's a skillful feat of boatmanship that guides us through this floating, tumbling mass and within an hour or so we manage to break out, clear, ahead of the ice. With the sun leaving us, and the cold creeping in, it's full speed for home.

The next morning, safely back at camp, Stephen shows me the traditional way to skin the caribou. It's an intricate process of butchery and there's very little waste. His daughter Margaret is in charge of the smoking house where we hang up all the meat. The spring hunt is vital to the Gwitchin as they can stock up on meat for the next few months, until the caribou, they hope, come through again in the autumn on their way south. It's a comforting sight to see the smoke house full of meat and there's a good feeling in the camp.

Like many First Nation Arctic communities, the Gwitchin are a naturally reserved and quiet people. But now that I've been here a few days Stephen is starting to open up and share some of his memories, and his anxieties. 'As you get older, of course you start to remember the old times. You miss the way we all used to go out hunting and then take our place round the fire while the old people would tell their stories. I miss those things. This is my country, I was brought up here. I consider myself native to the land, to everything. I get very emotional, or whatever you call it, when I hear the drilling might take place.'

CARIBOU The Reindeer of the European Arctic and the Caribou of Northern America – *rangifer tarandus* – are actually the same species. The name caribou derives from 'xalibu', which means 'pawer' in Mi'kmaq, Nova Scotian Native American, a reference to the animal's pawing in winter, digging through the snow and ice in search of food. Some herds of caribou travel more than 5,000 kilometres every year between winter feeding sites and the traditional calving grounds, where they gather in huge numbers on the shores of the polar sea. Their migration mirrors the movement of the 0°C isotherm, as this early thaw point heralds the most nutritious plants springing up. They also keep moving to try to find respite from the swarms of mosquitoes and to avoid the larger predators that feast on the herd, the wolves and brown bears rarely following them onto the tundra.

Though the sizes of caribou herds have risen and fallen in the past, the question today really is whether climate change has altered the environment in such as way that any recovery in numbers would be impossible. The Bathurst Arctic herd numbered 472,000 in 1986. Today, it is down to around 120,000. The Central Arctic herd had 17,500 animals in 1992 but now there are maybe less than 2,000. Over in Alaska, the Yukon and in Canada's Northwest Territories, the Porcupine caribou herd has declined from 178,000 animals in 1989 to the 120,000 or so that biologists counted the last time they were able to do a comprehensive census. Maybe there are only 100,000 today?

In places like the south-central coast of the Canadian Arctic, there are so few animals left that a recovery may never happen. Not only is this threatening the future of the lucrative sports hunt in the Yukon and Nunavut, it also

threatens to strike at the heart and soul of Inuit, Gwitchin, Dene and Métis cultures. In most communities, the measure of a hunter is judged by his skill in killing enough animals to feed not only his family but other members of the village who may not be healthy or old enough to go out on the land. A single caribou also saves a family $500 to $1,500 that they might otherwise have to spend on store-bought meat.

Climate changes are perhaps felt most keenly in the quality and abundance of food for the caribou itself. Some of their favoured lichens are being replaced by inedible plants in critical feeding grounds; elsewhere the changing density of the snow pack makes finding food difficult over the long bleak winters. Wetter weather in spring and autumn, followed by freezing, results in the icing over of food which compounds their struggle. The cool and remote coastal calving areas, which usually 'green up' just as the pregnant cows arrive in spring, are warming and it may be that they no longer provide relief from flies and predators. In Greenland, over-stressed caribou have been arriving on calving grounds as much as a month too late, when the changed nutritional value and digestibility is affecting calf survival.

The collapse of the caribou herds would have far-reaching impacts, a very real crisis because of their economic and cultural significance to the people of the Arctic. Adopting a language that may ensure their voices are heard, the Gwitchin now speak of the future of the caribou as a 'human rights issue'. As they continue to develop sustainability plans, they 'do this with the Porcupine herd not only in their minds but in their hearts'. They have real doubt that they can exist without the caribou.

Stephen's biggest fear is the loss of the caribou. Their calving grounds in Alaska are currently under threat from oil exploration and the Gwitchin people are fighting to protect their way of life. 'Our leaders, our elders from our community go down,' Robert adds, 'they go down lobbying the US government, pleading with them to stop thinking about drilling in the calving grounds. The more drilling there is, of course, it will disturb the caribou. It's a disaster happening day by day.' It seems obvious to me that this will cause problems for the old way of life, and for the health of the herd. Stephen believes it's important to keep asking the question, to keep challenging why this development is necessary. 'You know, the caribou can't talk for themselves, so we have to talk for them. Even though we kill them, and we eat them, they provide us, our families, with life, our way of life.'

Over the course of the next few days, we venture out on various hunting trips for food. The Gwitchin territory can provide a rich harvest of wildfowl and other animals, but it is the caribou that sustain their life here. Stephen has a wealth of knowledge about the wilderness and knows every square inch of the land around his cabin. And he doesn't like to go home empty handed. I'd be happy to stay out here with his family for longer than my short trip allows – for months in fact. Stephen is a gentle, funny and wonderful man. His doctor told him not to make this trip – he has been having heart problems and only has use of one lung. But it's an honour to spend some time with him. He regularly wakes me up, with a mug of coffee and a joke about being a lazy kid. We get up before the rest of the crew, so we can spend some time together. He knew I'd enjoy the mornings with him. We drink together, chat a little, enjoy the stillness.

He takes me on a few little jaunts around and about and, like an eager young pupil, I lap up lessons on traps, fox links, wolf and weasel snares, berries, medicine, gum, nests, flora and fauna. Stephen also began to talk a little bit about his life, his history. I hope so much that he will feel comfortable enough to talk to me about such delicate subjects as the identity of his people and the connection to nature. This could be such a wonderful programme if we could access such subjects gently in a respectful and non-patronizing way. We all have so much to learn about those feelings, beliefs, skills and truths that the old first nations of the Americas knew which haven't been stamped out, lost or forgotten. It seems so relevant in today's mad, industrial, consumer-driven world, and I would love the opportunity to learn more from my wonderful hosts. I need to keep trying.

18 MAY: PORCUPINE RIVER
Stephen and Margaret are taking me to a very special and private place for their family, a few miles down river towards Alaska. We decide to go ahead of the others and paddle the big aluminium canoe, away from the chug of outboard motors. The light

OPPOSITE : Nice beaver Stephen! I made this joke loads of times on camera, but it won't make the cut. The two of us went out on hunting trips alone, and he shared his knowledge of the land with me.

THIS PAGE: The sun slowly dips below the treeline. The spruce forest and willow thicket glow in the half light.
OVERLEAF: Stephen and I have many opportunities to share stories over a cup of coffee.

is golden, the forest and mountains stretch out before us. We eventually reach our destination — it's the old cabin where Stephen's parents brought him up, and it feels a great privilege to be allowed to come here. The edge of the forest creates a natural courtyard around the log shelter, its sides surrounded by tall grasses. It seems a tiny place, yet in his childhood the hut was shared between twelve — his parents and ten restless young children. It must have been a tough experience. 'Is it special? Of course,' he says, always eager to have a joke with me, 'but we're only looking at a goddamn old house, you know Bruce. That's just the way it was.'

Stephen's father was a white policeman who fell in love with a local Indian woman. As a Mountie, he wasn't able to continue the relationship unless he left the service, which he did so they could get married. Stephen's mother showed her husband how to survive in the wilderness and they home-taught all their children. In 1911 the Canadian Government had built a new boarding school for Indian children at Carcross. Stephen's mother had been enrolled there. It was the beginning of a difficult era for Yukon native people. The school often forcibly removed children from their families and kept them apart for months, sometimes years, at a time. The school's lessons were limited to basic writing and arithmetic, and a loyalty to Christianity and the British Empire was drummed into the children. Indian culture and traditions were considered irrelevant, subhuman even. Students, Stephen's mother included, were forbidden to speak their native languages. The teachers were mostly religious missionaries and the indoctrination was harsh. They were made to feel like savages and it is no surprise that this has left deep scars that may never fully heal.

There were cases of actual physical and sexual abuse, yet certainly so many more remain unrecorded, not talked about then, perhaps too painful to remember now. Cut adrift from their own culture, but not readily accepted by white society, many children left the school before graduation only to face new problems in trying

to adapt to life back in their home communities. By the late 1960s the Canadian Government had changed its policy of forced assimilation of native people into the mainstream and these residential schools were phased out. But the policy was entrenched. Whole generations of children missed their traditional upbringing and returned as strangers to their lands. Beliefs, attitudes, orals and aspirations had all been turned upside down. It was now seen as backward to consider the land as sacred. God lived in the sky and humans ruled over nature. From this standpoint, the land was ripe for manipulation. Much spirituality and knowledge was lost forever.

Stephen escaped the dark times of the residental schools, living in this small log cabin at the edge of the forest. It might sound idyllic, in comparison, but he hints there were times of deep hardship. He recalls the times his parents had scolded him for complaining about hunger. Though he knows that times must change for each generation, he hates the waste of the young kids today. He feels something important has been lost in the most recent generation, something big he feels has slipped away. He remembers the months they ran out of food, a life so close to starvation, but he doesn't want to dishonour his mother by dwelling too much on it – it's not always helpful looking back at the past. Times were hard, but the Gwitchin are a resourceful people, and they found a way to make a life within the forest and by the river. Nature provided for them, they learned to adapt. Stephen doesn't know his actual birthday but he thinks he's 78 years old. He was born in the old world, living the same life his mother's people had lived for many generations. But, more than ever before, the Arctic is changing. Now Stephen is one of the last of his kind.

The longer I'm here, the more I'm starting to understand the strength of the bond between the Gwitchin and the caribou. And it explains their growing fear that the delicate balance that has existed for millennia could soon be disrupted by the arrival of the oil industry. 'Nobody knows what exactly is going to happen,' Stephen

THESE PAGES: Stephen gets to work in the smoke house. It might look like a lot of meat, but this will last a number of families until the caribou return.

says, as we share food together one last time. 'Maybe nothing will happen, but they're scared. I get scared, you know. When you start playing with nature you're fighting a big war and we're the ones that are going to lose. You know, some people might get a few dollars, but if the caribou are gone, well, they might as well come and kill us all too. We feel that the herd is not as big, not as healthy as it used to be. If it's not hunters that are doing it, then you have to look to bigger reasons. Maybe, you look to that thing climate change, you look to the way the environment is changing.'

Today is our last full day and no one is in a rush to leave. Rob, my director, thinks that he accidentally deleted a whole camera disc last night. I feel awful for him, so I'd better start scribbling or we'll have no record of what we've done. Yesterday we went off to the hunting lake called Goose Camp, in search of more game. I'd been bought some wellies, in anticipation of the marsh we had to cross, but they were at least four sizes too big. This meant only one thing, huge suction with not enough foot traction to get my little legs out. Even speed, which is the usual trick in traversing such a bog, wasn't good enough. With limbs tiring and laden with heavy gear (I had a rifle and the big camera) I was completely useless and it was pretty much the same for every-

one. So much for heroic adventure: nature quickly brought us to our knees. One of our crew, Zubin, had forgotten to bring wellies and we'd given him a right teasing until we realized that going barefoot was a better option than complete immobility, floundering in our boots. It was one of those comical moments when filming goes to pot because the crew are unable to operate, a bunch of grown men laughing in tears, wallowing in glorious mud.

Our screams and the frantic snapping of twigs to try and make some sort of bridging road meant that by the time we arrived at the lake there was nothing left there at all. No surprise. The spectacle was worth the lack of results, although it's a shame not to have a conclusion to the scene. After Goose Camp we went to the lake near the main camp to see if there were any more geese to be had. There was a wide cut path from the river to another part of the lake, a pathway through the forest that Stephen had made in years past. Cut paths always make a stalk much easier which is why they're so common. Our newly silent approach was rewarded by a number of ducks close to the lake, but none good for eating so they were left alone. I made my way back to Bluefish Camp by another trail.

THESE PAGES: Out with the boys on a duck hunt, rifles at the ready. It's not easy travelling quietly through this wilderness with a film crew and tons of gear following you around.

I went to Peter's cabin for the first time last night, a modern hunter's pad for sure, quite unexpected out here so close to nature. Every surface seems varnished, inside and out, an open-plan kitchen with metal and plastic windows and expensive fittings, almost like an ideal home. The space was filled with music, home-brew beer (which was quite strong by all accounts) and weaponry in abundance. Rifles, axes, saws and shotguns proudly gathered like china ornaments arranged on a mantelpiece or side table. We decided to hang out in the camp to do some final general filming, chopping wood to add to the supply for next year, collecting water, drying the final bits of meat and fixing paths before we left this place.

I was able to spend another afternoon with Stephen. We talked about religion, animism, and the problems of modern life, all the while tending his small vegetable garden: his white father's influence, he tells me, a domestic addition to the usual hunting and trapping existence. We put in peas, cauliflowers and carrots, rows of cabbages and radishes and it was good to be away from the cameras.

His tenderness and his friendship I value highly, even though we have spent barely a couple of weeks together. It felt very much like being with a grandfather I'd never met. He has taught me a lot. I'm so pleased he made it out to his camp, despite being told he was too ill to come. He thinks it may be his last visit, but we continue to plant the seeds for next year all the same. Life goes on, he says gently. I begin to cry.

22 MAY: OLD CROW

It's time to leave camp and head back to Old Crow with our meat. This hunt has provided Stephen and his family with enough food for the next four months so he's
feeling pretty happy. We're heading back to the ramshackle village for a series of
special events: the annual spring festival, known as 'Caribou Days'. Everyone has
returned from hunting, and the villagers are gathering to celebrate the return of some
of the caribou and to share their success. Each family takes about five caribou in the
spring, and donates part of it to the festival.

The first event is the muskrat skinning competition. The Gwitchin are the
northernmost people of a much bigger group known as the Athabascan Indians, and
they are possibly the most traditional. All the contests help to develop the skills
needed for the old way of life, hunting and trapping in the wilderness. As skinned car-
casses pile up on the picnic benches, down by the riverside, it makes me laugh: not
like the village fête back home, with our tea and cakes. Later on, third prize in the log-
sawing contest wins me $10 and I'm chuffed to bits.

It was nice to be back in Old Crow, although it felt so disjointed and busy after
our week of relative solitude in the forest. One of my appointments was to meet
Donald Russell, one of the world's leading experts on caribou, scientifically speaking,
who was going to come with us on a flight over the area spotting the migration the
following day. He came for dinner and we ate together in our guest house. Friday was

flight day and we all got up super early because the pilot was expected at 7 a.m. to avoid the turbulence that comes from the hot air rising from the heated land. However, our pilot didn't come until the afternoon, so much of the day was spent waiting around. It's quite usual in these parts and the pilot, when he finally pitched up, didn't even gesture an apology.

I was frustrated of course, but took the chance to go and visit Stephen. He was pleased to see me and we just pottered around his house, doing odd jobs and working the soil in his village garden. I had heard from more than a few people back in town that Stephen is going to Vancouver next week for a heart bypass, a difficult operation, and that it was an unspoken possibility that the trip to his cabin would be his last. Like the vegetables we planted together, I really hope Stephen will be going strong next year. I wonder if I may have a chance to see him again.

Later that afternoon, when we finally get airborne, the views are stunning. We head north over the Crow Flats, a vast area of land littered with hundreds of lakes, some many miles wide, a patterned mosaic of reflected sunlight. Those lakes to the south were water, and as we moved further north they became small jewels of ice. We

flew to the mountains just before the Arctic sea but there was no sign of the caribou, just endless, bare tundra and only a few patches of snow, which surprised Don and the pilot who expressed how unseasonal it was. I had a good chance to question Don on the area and the caribou herds worldwide.

Surprisingly, he didn't think that global warming was overly affecting the herd at the moment. The fifty-year cycle in numbers was bigger than the warming of the area, in fact warmer temperatures leading to less snow could be beneficial. It was the change-able, often extreme, weather that was making life difficult, more unpredictable. Freezing layers of ice over snow made it hard for the herd to access the lichen. Don accepts that no one fully knows what exactly is going on with the caribou. Climate change, human activities and industrial development are all likely playing a role. So perhaps are con-taminants which are creeping into the animals' food supply. It is no simple picture.

In fact, part of the problem, although to a lesser extent now that survey tech-niques have improved, is finding enough animals to get an accurate estimate of how many caribou there are. During two days of flying with our experts we only manage to see twelve caribou. On other days, with more luck, certainly we'd have seen many more. Even a good count in a year when weather and migratory animals cooperate, Don says, has a possibility of error of plus or minus 10 per cent. The size of the range of some of the herds is simply too big to get a more accurate count economically. And there's always the possibility that a migration route or calving ground site has shifted before or during a census. Theoretically, that could increase the element of doubt over actual numbers to much higher levels. Scientists 'have come to realize that the biggest reason for these ebbs and flows lie in a complex relationship between the caribou's ability to find food and its ability not to be food.'

BELOW: Some of the rivers are swollen with spring snow melt and the remains of the winter ice.
OVERLEAF: Others, like this tributary of the Porcupine are still and ice free.

THIS PAGE: From the beautiful forest to an industrial waste-land – welcome to the Tar Sands of Alberta.

Yet, other people I had spoken to in Old Crow have been quick to shout about the loss of the caribou here. They called for regulation; but some were also unwilling to agree that improved hunting methods – high-calibre rifles, speedy motorboats, quad bikes and skidoos – have in any way adversely damaged the state of the herd. Overall it isn't a simple story, some herds in other parts of the world are actually increasing in number while the Porcupine climaxed in 1990 at 180,000. It would be reasonable to suggest, however, that if temperatures do continue to rise this will ultimately be negative to the caribou, and the ecosystems of which they are a central part. To replace the meat for those that live off the herd would cost an estimated $20 million a year in imported food.

The caribou harvest sustains Old Crow, all year round. All other food has to be flown in here at great cost, so having a supply of local meat is a lifeline to the community. And it helps to build up our energy for the evening ahead – my last night here. Perhaps surprisingly, the Gwitchin people are very keen on jigging. They learned the custom from Scottish fur trappers in the nineteenth century and took to it with gusto. The Scots have long gone or settled elsewhere, but the dancing lives on, and continues late into the night. Having felt like a bit of a wallflower, finally I plucked up courage and asked Stephen's grand-daughter Sam for a spin. She tires me out long before the music stops. Jigging, log-chopping, skinning and singing – a real Arctic community party – but central to this celebration is the caribou. It's a festival for the caribou, in honour of them providing for the village as the summer begins to close. The respect and love for this animal is everywhere, despite what an outsider might think when

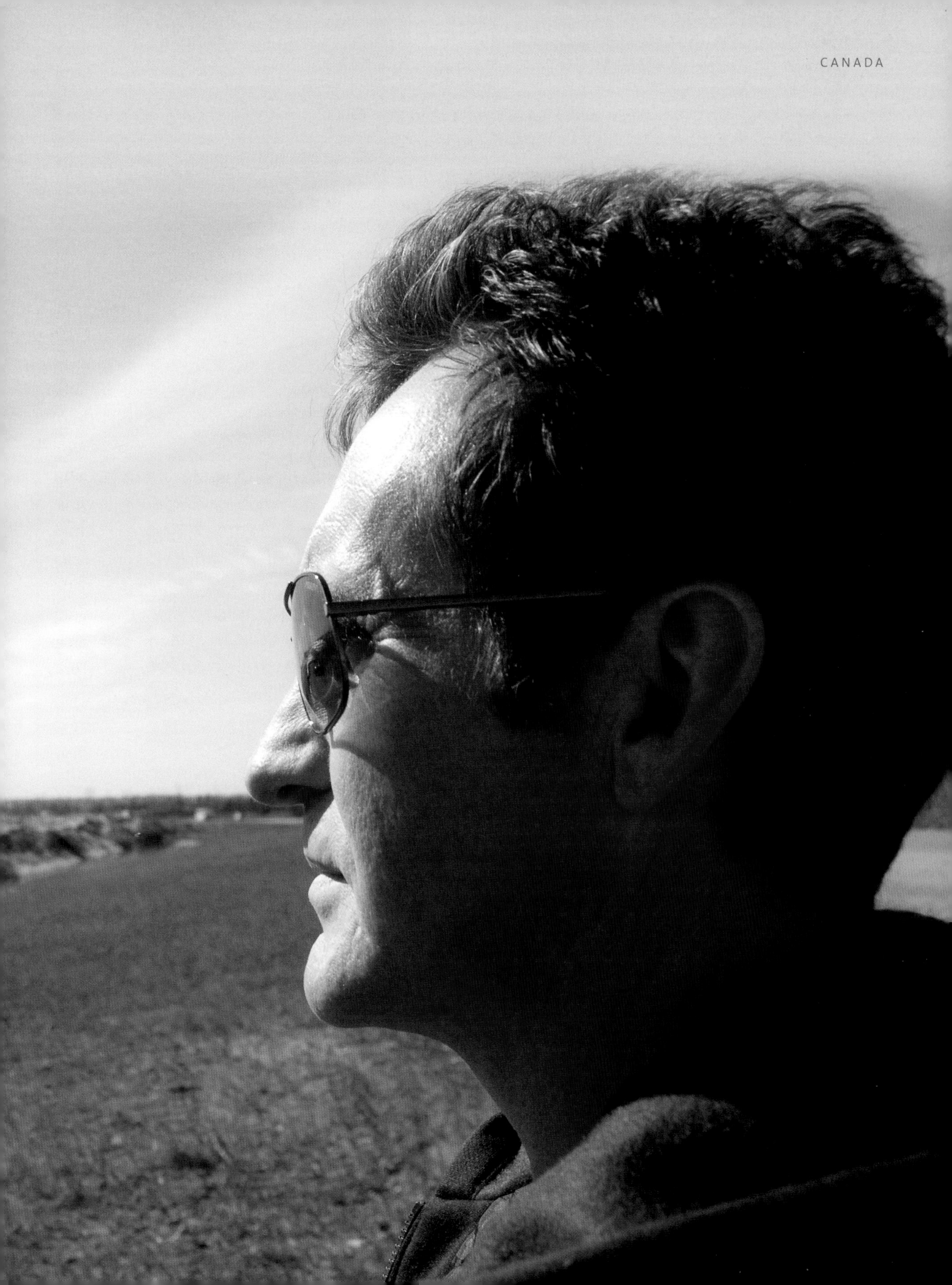

ABOVE: Once a birch-bark canoe, now a shiny new speed-boat: Chief Jim Boucher takes me on a tour of his tribal lands. OPPOSITE: Beneath the green sweep of boreal forest lie potential riches, the bitumen tar sands that can be refined into petroleum products. The tall chimneys of the tar sands processing plant compete with nature.

seeing the butchery of the hunt. They teach their children to honour the caribou too, and that respect is central to their relationship with the natural world.

I hope these people get to decide their own future, but the forces of development are looming on the horizon. Tomorrow I'm leaving to go and meet another group of Athabascan Indians who also used to hunt and trap in the wilderness for thousands of years, until the oil industry arrived on their doorstep.

24 MAY: ATHABASCA RIVER

I'm travelling 2,000 kilometres southeast of Old Crow, some way below the Arctic Circle to the Tar Sands of northern Alberta, the single largest industrial emitter of carbon dioxide gases on the planet. The Tar Sands stretch across an area the size of England, and contain the second largest proven oil reserves in the world after Saudi Arabia. As our helicopter surveys this tragic wasteland, a vista of utter desolation, despair and sadness well in the pit of my stomach. Vast areas of pristine wilderness have been ripped up for the extraction of oil from within the sand here, a region now producing 1.3 million barrels a day. In a world wracked by fears of diminishing oil reserves and safety issues, particularly with deepwater offshore drilling, the Canadian Tar Sands offer a safer alternative. Production is now set to double in the next ten years and will continue for decades.

But it comes at a massive cost to the environment, and to the indigenous peoples who live in this area. As I travel to meet them, a pall seems to hang over the land, a smell that's pungent and acrid. It's very thick, it's not pleasant, and it's everywhere. I learn that it comes and goes on the wind, but nonetheless today was particularly bad. I set out on the Athabasca River which flows though the heart of the Tar Sands. I'm travelling in a speedboat with Jim Boucher, Chief of the Fort McKay First Nation, who's seen a lot of changes during his time as leader. Like most people here, he grew up hunting, gathering and trapping. 'In the old days, you could take a cup, reach out over the boat and drink it.' How about now, I ask? 'Nowadays,' he says, matter-of-factly, 'people would rather drink poison.'

'We used to have a very spiritual connection to the land, to life here and the animals. Everyone was involved in hunting and trapping. That was the way of life for many generations and for a long time people were adamant they wanted to continue and maintain that life,' he describes. But in the 1970s the oil industry arrived and the landscape changed dramatically. We turn with a bend in the river, and the forest gives way to a nightmarish vision of mines, oil pipelines and pylons; smoke, metal and concrete. It's deeply depressing. It's noisy, smelly, dirty, wasteful, not at all like the Arctic Circle I have enjoyed over the last few months. It feels like the end of the world.

At first Jim's people tried to oppose the industry, but the government claimed ownership of their land and minerals, and has now sold oil leases to over ninety companies. In the early days the local people were not consulted when the prospectors turned up. Jim's grandfather's cabin was bulldozed with all his possessions still in it – rifles, tents, rods, stove and bedding ground into the mud. No one even knew it had happened until they came back from a hunt. Trapping lines were destroyed and homes flattened. The community tried to protest, blockades were erected, petitions signed, lawyers engaged, but nothing came of it. 'We had no chance on Earth to stop this going on,' Jim relates.

'It was a decision made to the south of here by a white government and we had absolutely no say in terms of what went on then.' What happened next would change the fortunes of the locals forever. Jim and his people decided to do business with the industry and turned an environmental disaster into a golden economic opportunity.

They set up a group of companies owned by the community to provide support services to the industry and before long became involved in fuel distribution, reclamation, haulage, and warehousing. So, as well as being chief of his people, Jim is now the head of a multi-million dollar business empire. Chief Boucher is Chairman of the Board of the Fort McKay Group, operating six limited companies, 100 per cent owned and controlled by First Nation peoples, in addition to other joint venture partnerships they are exploring. Under Jim's leadership, the Group has grown into one of the most successful indigenous-owned business ventures in Canada, boasting fixed assets and annual revenues in excess of $200 million. It's a vast enterprise and the pace of change here now almost defies belief.

Jim is smiling as he reels off these stats, joking that when he was growing up all he really owned was a dog team. I ask him, having fought so hard against development here, how it feels to be so involved in the development and, ultimately, the devastation of his ancestral lands? 'It's not what our ancestors might have wanted, or could have imagined, but ultimately we want to ensure that our community is healthy and that it has a future. If we don't become part of the mainstream economy, well, it means that we're sitting on the sidelines in poverty. That's just not an option for our community.' The tribe has struck a bargain, they have voiced their concerns and set their own agenda, and although it may well be a deal with the devil, I wonder what alternative they may have had. It must have been a tough time.

On two different sites, the Fort McKay Group also runs accommodation and catering for over 3,000 oil workers. The camp is a multi-ethnic melting pot of people from all over the world, as the Tar Sands boom offers the chance to earn a lot of money very quickly: if you work weekends and overtime, you can make $1,000 a day. The nearby town of Fort McMurray is where the workers go to let off steam and spend some of their hard-earned cash. There's a jaded, almost inhuman detachment in the voices of many of the workers, when I ask them about the industry.

They're not embarrased to admit that the money is the only thing attracting them here, neither the land nor the people are of much interest to these guys. Are they ashamed? 'No way, I've never heard anyone at home complain about it. If it wasn't for us nobody would be driving cars, everyone would be riding around in electric vehicles.' Wouldn't that be a good thing, I ask? 'As long as the world has a dependancy on oil, most people couldn't care less about where it comes from – though some might bitch about every aspect of it.' 'As long as we can make a good living out of it, no problem,' agrees another, as we chat together over dinner. Fort McMurray is enjoying

OPPOSITE: Once-vibrant forest is reduced to these open pits. The oil industry strip mines and drills to get at the bitumen that lies under the trees. This thick material is then separated, thinned down and piped out for refining into gasoline and diesel. In this process large tracts of forest and wetland habitat are lost forever.

its boom time, but it has no appeal for me. All the outsiders are here for one thing alone – money. But the price of development seems to me too high. Nature is the provider and the victim. I wonder how long it will take before we realize this.

26 MAY: FORT MCMURRAY

With a population of 70,000 migrant workers, mostly men, the town feels pretty grim and soulless and I'm really missing the hunters of Old Crow. But we're in town to make a film and so we pick ourselves up for tomorrow. Fort McMurray wasn't as bad as I was expecting at all. I'd heard about thick smog enveloping the town, drugs and social unrest, absolute desolation in the surrounding countryside and more. First impressions were that the boreal forest was absolutely beautiful, still a welcome presence standing beyond this little enclave of concrete, bright lights and pick-up trucks. Flying in, the forest still stretched for miles and miles.

There were certainly no casinos and burger joints when the first outsiders came here in search of furs over 200 years ago. A Hudson's Bay Company trading post was established by 1870 and the town grew slowly into the next century, part of the white man's cash economy, but its people were always at the edge. But all that changed when the oil men came. Trembling aspen, white spruce, birch and poplar still stand tall, though traffic lights and electricity pylons now sprawl downtown in their place. One of the advantages about meeting Jim Boucher is that he has such a close working relationship with the oil companies here. He's managed to get permission for us to go and meet some of the workers on site, which as film-makers we'd never normally be able to access. Fort McKay First Nation runs a haulage business on the Shell-owned Albian Sands surface mine, and Jim has arranged for me to meet one of his truck drivers to go for a tour around the facility.

I was expecting to meet a burly sort of bloke, with hairy arms and well-invested beer belly, so you can imagine my delight when my truck driver Patricia turned up.

Our tour bus for the morning is one of Jim's 100-ton monster vehicles. We're off on one of Patricia's regular runs, hauling dirt from a newly cleared area to a man-made mountain at the other end of the site. They are building themselves a mountain with this post-industrial mud. Patricia is a single mother, so she needs to work here to support her three young kids. She can see herself doing the job for a long time, the money is good and she would like to move up in the business. I ask her if she worries about the environmental cost, if people in the community are troubled by the big industry happening here? 'Well, Bruce, the issues with wildlife, that's the only risk I can see. Other than that, no. You know what I mean, this is the way that we support our families, this is the way of living right now. This is all that we have around us.'

Patricia is a member of the Fort McKay First Nation and her family have been hunting and trapping here for generations. Her grandmother grew up in the forest. I ask Patricia what her family thinks of all this. 'She's old, you know. My grandma will never know what's fully going on here. I'm sure they don't tell all the elders exactly what's going on, how much pollution and damage is being done here,' Patricia says with a shrug. 'As soon as they just wave a bit of money, the problems go away for a while, it keeps them quiet for a bit, right.' Patricia is rational. Who am I to tell her

THESE PAGES: The tar sands processing plants are a blight on the landscape. Expanding the industry here also requires building a huge network of pipelines and refineries.
OVERLEAF: The bitumen tar sands cannot by pumped from the ground like conventional oil, but must be mined. Massive machines dig up the earth and load it into trucks the size of houses.

what she should or shouldn't be doing with her life. She has every reason to be guarded when she speaks to me and, having met so many officials now, I respect her straightforward honesty when she talks. I ask her if it makes her sad. 'Of course, I just wish I was a lawyer or something, so I could get right in there and really try to understand what's going on. I don't really understand it fully myself. If I did, I don't know. I think if I really understood maybe I'd want to do something about it. But you can't fight this industry, you know what I mean? You'd be crazy if you did.'

Crazy certainly, but without challenge, without asking questions of these industries, I can't see any hope for the environment here, or in fact, hope for elsewhere on our planet. It is madness that we keep plundering the way we do, driven only by money, fuelling our modern lifestyles. This is also the present for the Indians here, and I'll admit right now there doesn't seem to be a second way. There is certainly no going back.

Tar Sands oil is known as dirty oil. Extracting it from the bitumen soaked sand requires huge amounts of energy and has only become profitable in the last decade, due to rising oil prices and new technology. The oil-laden dirt is carved from the earth and after some six days of processing, the extracted oil is good enough to go into your car. It takes one barrel of oil to produce two barrels from the Tar Sands

OPPOSITE: Each massive truck carries about 300 tons of soil per load to an extraction plant, where a hot water process separates the bitumen from the sand and other minerals.
ABOVE: Downtown Fort McMurray. Casinos, motels, bright lights, and traffic. I'm miserable.

ABOVE: A small section of forest is preserved as it once was across the whole region. But don't be fooled: just beyond the river, the trees have been cut down.

OPPOSITE: In the middle of this is Chief Jim's cabin. We visited for a short while. I try hard to imagine what it must have been like here for his father. I am left feeling so guilty about the damage we do to our planet.

and yet the profits are still enormous. This is staggering, excessive, and it should frighten us all. If all the costs were born into the equation, not to mention the gross subsidies that support the business, then it simply would not be viable. It makes me feel troubled and confused. Just how long can we let this go on?

28 MAY: FORT McKAY

The Tar Sands industry literally never sleeps. These trucks are busy hauling sand 24 hours a day, 365 days a year and will continue to do so until it all runs out, in about 200 years time. God knows what our planet will be like then if development like this continues or even takes off within the Arctic Circle. In the middle of all this desolation is a small reminder of how things used to be. Jim has a hunting cabin that belonged to his father that is still standing. It's a small haven at the heart of the extraction site.

'I built my dad's cabin many years ago, when there was no mine here, just bush,' he tells me as we make our way past the machinery and pipelines that now disfigure the area. To get to Jim's cabin these days he has to pass through a security checkpoint,

THESE PAGES: Tar sands are a combination of clay, sand, water and bitumen – a heavy, thick hyrocarbon with the consistency of tar. The largest deposits in the world are here, south of the Canadian Arctic.

and we're accompanied by a convoy of PR and safety people from the Shell oil company. The throb and smell of the mine site reaches out to us through the small screen of trees. Fifteen years ago there was no sign of man here at all, just forest. 'Yeah, there was nothing here. Just squirrels and rabbits, beaver, muskrat, fish, ducks and geese.' Now, a film crew, a convoy of trucks, and not far away is the mine, the constant, ominous presence. Jim is pleased to be here, but I can tell the memories of the way this land once was are painful to him, no matter how materially successful and wealthy his people have become. It's the second time during my visit to Canada that I've visited an old family cabin, but this time is very different to Stephen's parents' place out on the river near Old Crow.

We stop to have quite a strange barbecue with all the oil people. Jim's older sister Rose is cooking up moose and caribou and clearly hasn't read the script. 'Look at the land now,' she tells me, beyond earshot of the rest of the crowd. 'The land had been raped, that's how I feel. Mother Earth has been raped, simple as that. The trees have been cut down, things are being taken out of the land, which will not be put back properly. The water has been abused. The animals are being abused. Where will they go? They won't return here that's for sure. It's our land, my father's land, and we should have access to it, you know. I believe in progress, to try to make things better for our community, but not to totally erase what was there before, not to totally erase a whole way of life, a whole nation, just for progress? No, I don't think so.'

I've always thought of Canada as a fairly liberal and green country but instead of reducing their greenhouse emissions, they're increasing them exponentially, with the Tar Sands accounting for half of that increase. Toxic waste sits in vast tailings ponds, potentially seeping into the water system, downstream to Lake Athabasca and out into the Arctic Ocean. Some communities living downstream have developed rare forms of cancer which they claim is due to industrial pollution, but the government and the oil companies deny this. In the spring a few years ago almost a thousand migrating ducks landed on one of those tailings ponds, at a newer Syncrude 'Aurora' mine north of Fort McKay. They never left its oily surface. The incident stirred public outrage and it spilled over into the international media – Greenpeace broke into the Syncrude facility and hoisted a banner of a skull over the pipe discharging tailings, along with a sign that read: 'World's Dirtiest Oil: Stop the Tar Sands'. The company is still embroiled in a court case about these toxic ponds and, rightly, the focus on the operations here has never been so intense. It seems clear to me though, that nature will always be the victim. So much damage happens here and elsewhere, on a daily basis,

OPPOSITE: My host, Jim Boucher, Chief of the Fort McKay First Nation, feels a connection to the past but his work has taken his people into the heart of the industry here. He is now head of a multi-million dollar business empire. 'The old way of life is gone,' he tells me, 'and we will never be able to bring it back.'
OVERLEAF: Most of us think of Canada as clean and wild. It may come as a shock to learn that what Environmental Defence, a Canadian organization, has called 'the most destructive project on Earth' is happening here.

when we are not looking. I shudder to think what happens around our planet, beyond the reach of cameras and protesters, on the edge and beyond our conscience.

Despite these undoubted environmental dangers, the economic benefits are plain to see. At Jim's village, Fort McKay, they spent $40 million last year on new facilities and every man, woman and child in the tribe gets $10,000 a year automatically as a share of the profits. And the cash just keeps rolling in. Fort McKay is now looking to start its own oil extraction company. Every house in the village is now a modern detached home with a big car in the drive, some with speedboats parked out front. The community centre is a multi-million-dollar modern building, and nearby are the Fort McKay First Nation offices, which are already too small. There is an elders' daycare centre with riverside views. The community has every modern convenience an outsider might think it needs, with a free gym, picnic sites, online schooling classrooms, playgroups and a golf driving range. Outside Jim's headquarters complex, there are new trees planted between the windows, so inside there's a glimpse of some greenery from every view.

Among the trappings of corporate success in Jim's office, his traditional headdress stands out as a symbol of the past. He happily wears it for me, leaning back on his imitation-leather executive chair, as we chat a little and try to make sense of what path his people might take in the future. The desktop screen image on his office computer shows a sweeping green field, a Windows vision of the world, but it's a dream long since past. 'I would prefer we had the old way of life, but the simple fact of the matter is the old way of life is gone. It died with my grandfather. It died with our ancestors. It died when oil was first produced from the ground in this region and we will never be able to bring it back.' He spoke slowly and clearly. It was shocking to hear.

Hunting caribou in the wilderness near Old Crow feels like a long way away from here. I've met two very different men on this trip, leading very different lives. Jim has embraced the future, but Stephen is still living in the past, and embodies a way of life that's disappearing from large parts of the Arctic. You could say Chief Jim sold out, but given the circumstances, it's hard to know what else the people of Fort McKay could have done. It would be so convenient to just blame everyone working here for all the damage that's happening, but really it's more complex than that. We are all to blame – anyone who's using oil in some way or other. Heading down the highway in a rented gas-guzzling truck, giving my thoughts on this to camera, I realize I'm as much a part of the problem as many others. It's our addiction to oil that's driving the economy, that's driving what's happening here and until that changes this sort of thing is going to continue. I'm part of the problem and need to be an example somehow. Can I do it?

The Arctic undoubtedly harbours massive wealth and Canada understandably wants to make the most of its resources. But the pace of development here is rampaging and the values which support it don't seem to take account of everything that's being lost in the process.

THE TAR SANDS

In Canada, the oil industry is transforming boreal forests and wetlands – one of the world's last remaining virgin ecosystems – into 'America's gas tank'. Alberta's forest is home to a diverse range of animals, including beavers, lynx, caribou and grizzly bears, as well as providing breeding grounds for many North American songbirds and waterfowl. Oil companies are scraping up hundreds of thousands of acres of this wildlife haven to mine 'tar sands' – the silty deposits that contain crude bitumen.

These sands lay relatively untouched for much of the twentieth century, when oil was plentiful and available elsewhere. It was simply too expensive and inconvenient to extract it. In recent years, not least with oil insecurity in the Middle East, spiralling prices and a seemingly unquench-able domestic demand, the oil companies have turned their attentions north. In 2003, 30 square kilometres of land had been disturbed by tar sands development. By the summer of 2006, that number had grown to 2,000 square kilometres, an almost five-fold increase in just three years. The current process limit of 2.7 million barrels of oil per day is estimated to increase to 6 million barrels each day by 2030. Today, the tar sands represent around half of Canada's total oil production, and over 99 per cent of this exported crude goes to the USA for refining, through a network of more than 10,000 miles of pipeline.

Mining and drilling tar sands, extracting bitumen and turning it into crude oil is a dirty, destructive and energy-intensive process. It takes 4 tons of material dug out of open pit mines to produce a single barrel of oil; the amount

of natural gas used by the industry every day is enough to heat an estimated 4 million American homes. The production facilities, including pit mines, wells, roads and pipes, damage the forest's highly complex natural balance leaving an industrial moonscape behind. Smokestacks belch emissions into the atmosphere. Toxins and carcinogens are potentially bleeding into the water system.

If this wasn't bad enough, the production of synthetic crude oil from tar sands causes three times the global warming pollution of conventional crude oil production. The rush to strip-mine and exploit tar sands is destroying and fragmenting millions of acres of this wild forest for low-grade petroleum fuel, to satisfy our demand to drive our cars and travel the world by plane and meeting our needs when we leave our computers on at night. Right now there's nothing like oil, there's no other way to fly and that's why we are addicted to it. But sooner or later it will all run out.

The tar sands of Alberta have become the international oil industry's test site. If it proves acceptable to finance them, then the global finance sector will have normalized a disastrously high-carbon path of development. Many of our UK banks, some government funded, are contributing significant sums of corporate finance to underwrite this development because, of course, the potential profits are massive. But the long-term cost to our planet is incalculable. We still have to consider what to do when the tar sands run out. Why not do it now? It is not alarmist to begin to feel fearful about the temptation of the oil that lies beneath the forest floor.

SIBERIA

Siberia
SPIRITS IN THE LAND

'There is real spiritual depth here, but only now we are beginning our journey.'

It's the middle of summer and it feels like the middle of nowhere: Siberia. This vast, untamed wilderness of the Russian North stretches far into the Arctic. It's a place of extremes and is home to many indigenous people who endure such tough conditions with skill and ease. It's twenty years since the iron rule of the Soviet Union ended and the people of this region are only just beginning to rediscover their ancient traditions. I'm travelling from the city centres to the most remote encampments in the wild Verkhoyansk Mountains to see how the old ways are forging a new future. There is also a personal reason why this journey is so important to me. I've spent years living with tribal peoples, meeting their medicine men and, through trance, have journeyed into the spirit world. This region of Russia is where the word 'shaman' actually originates. What, if anything, will I find of these ancient spiritual beliefs?

Russia is the largest landmass in the Arctic. Stretching across nine time zones, it's home to some forty different indigenous peoples. I'm on my way to meet the Sakha, the 'horse people' of the Russian North. They live in the eastern state of Yakutia, otherwise known as the Sakha Republic. A vast region – some 3 million square kilometres – it's almost the size of India. If Sakha were an independent country, it would be the eighth largest in the world. Yet, for so vast a region, it has fewer than 950,000 inhabitants. India in comparison, I jot in my journal, is now home to over a billion people, one great mass of humanity. In the valleys of Siberia we will be almost alone, with just a few herders and a couple of thousand reindeer for company.

OVERLEAF: The city of Yakutsk in the Russian far east, is located just south of the Arctic Circle. The capital of the Sakha Republic, it is a major port on the Lena River. Though huge wealth has been generated by gold and diamond mining in the area, most of the city's people are poor. A statue of Lenin still greets visitors in the central square. It's the middle of summer, the sunlight catches the polished spires of the church. But in winter this is perhaps the coldest city on the planet. Everything is wrapped in snow and darkness, with temperatures regularly plummeting to minus 40°C.

Despite its enormous size, for many people Siberia remains a mystery. It's a place that seems to linger at the edge of the imagination; a region of ice floes and mighty rivers, endless bogs, nameless mountains, coal mines and oil fields, from which the remains of mammoths sometimes emerge from the permafrost. A bleak thread of railways, perhaps, ranks of contorted metal freezing in rusty hulks, a wilderness littered with the ghosts of the gulag prison camps and unspeakable horrors of the past. Officially, I'm told, there is no such place as Siberia. No political entity uses the name. In my atlas at home, the word marches across the northern third of Asia, sprawling and unconnected, as if resisting control. During Soviet times, revised maps erased the name entirely, in order to dispel Siberian regionalism. For a while, the people of Siberia were invisible to the world. They are now, gradually, turning again towards the sun.

18 June: Yakutsk

I'm arriving right in the middle of the Sakha festival season. It's nearing summer solstice, the longest day of the year, and one of the most important times for all of the peoples of the Far North. Here in Siberia, although celebrations to mark the solstice were outlawed under the old regime, there's now something of a revival. Under Soviet rule all indigenous religious beliefs were suppressed. For the Sakha people, the Yakuts, this meant the loss of their pagan sun festivals and the suppression of their shaman spirit guides; some say their wholesale extermination.

More than half of the Arctic land mass is in Russia, yet due to filming costs and permit restrictions we're only planning one episode of five in this vast area. I've been to northern Russia once before, travelling in the middle of winter to the Yamal Peninsula. For a number of weeks I followed the Nenets, hunting and herding on the tundra and learning a little of their nomadic way of life. Yamal translates as the 'end of the land' in the language of the native Nenets. Currently the region accounts for almost 90 per cent of Russia's gas production, and the extraction of huge untapped deposits threatens to transform vast expanses of tundra pasture into an industrial wasteland. We considered going back to explore their stories some more. But, there is so much of Russia to see, so much that doesn't reach audiences in the West, so we have come to the Sakha region instead. I'm travelling with Gavin Searle, the director for this episode, who I'm excited to be seeing again since working together on *Tribe*, living with the Layap yak-herders high in the mountains of Bhutan and the persecuted Penan of Sarawak. Joining our crew here is Florian Stammler, an anthropologist who taught us so much in the Yamal.

We cross the mighty Lena River by slow ferry then rejoin the dusty road. In winter, this river is frozen solid all the way to the Arctic Ocean, providing a rapid highway for truckers sending supplies to various outposts. Travel at that time is inhumanly cold but in many ways much easier than in the swampy, sweltering heat of high

summer. We pile into a ramshackle fleet of off-road vans – looking a little like jacked-up VW campers in battleship grey – which lurch down the dirt tracks as if there's no tomorrow. I want one desperately to tackle the rough roads at home. We are housed in a local school building for the night, chaperoned by its young master, his new shoes and rayon suit fresh for our cameras. We feast that evening on fried herring swimming in berries and cream. The following day we reach Balyktakh, a Sakha village that today is more famous for its fish than its horses. I'm meeting Alexander Sergeevich Artemiev or 'Kulan' as he is called by those who know his work. He's one of the new generation of local leaders who has emerged in recent years. He's an apostle for the new spirituality, the reconnecting to the old ways.

ABOVE LEFT: Dancing girls at the solstice festival smile for our camera.

ABOVE RIGHT: I don't really understand everything that's going on, but we're having fun.

In today's Russia of privatized health care, Kulan is in great demand as a healer. Gavin is constantly on transmit, funny, compassionate and charming, but full force. Our timings are tight and we are always behind, rushing everyone in our circle around at our behest. Always late and always frantic. Ever since hearing about Kulan, I knew that he had some magical gifts of knowledge to impart and I desperately wanted him to feature in our film, but there was a danger we would scare him off.

He takes me into a field beside the village to assess my wellbeing. He pulls a small instrument from his pocket and begins to play. The *vargan* mouth harp conveys the emotion of its player by imitating the sound of nature. This ancient instrument was banned under Stalin because of its links to shamanism. In the modern Russia, Kulan is now free to speak his *vargan* music to me, in an effort to diagnose my state of health. I can feel the vibrations of the *vargan* surge through my body. Really I can, it's quite a funny feeling. He reads that the left side of my body is 'weak', dark and vulnerable. I'm a little shocked as he's correct. How could he know? He pulls my muscles and they hurt, no surprise after so many weeks on the road. He uses a traditional Sakha horse-hair whisk to sense my energies and, he says, 'to clean my aura'. I am to let nature repair me. He leaves me lying amongst the grasses.

The summer solstice is a time of festivals. Kulan invites me to one of the biggest events of the year, the *Ysyakh*, a two-day holiday of fertility, renovation and rebirth. It starts with chalices of *kumys*, or fermented mare's milk, passed around and shared among the crowd. It tastes a little like off-yoghurt, but it's actually quite delicious. I sit in the shade of a tent and listen to some folk tales. Nearby an *olonkho* singer performs for a small crowd of old women – an *olonkho* is a heroic epic tale of the Sakha people that can vary between 10,000 and 20,000 verses. In the field behind me a few young men are stick fighting, and an old man is demonstrating Yakut archery. Boys wrestle beside the muddy path, bets are placed and spirits swilled.

During the Soviet era the festival was banned and instead became a showcase for the athletic prowess of the state. It was only in the 1990s that the villagers were once again allowed to return to their storytelling, chanting and dances. Beautifully dressed as white cranes, girls wheel in circles as if swooping over the treetops. At turns, the tannoy overhead pumps a stream of sharp orders and loud music, energizing the scene and directing the crowd to the next entertainment. It appears a strange mix of old and new, of half-remembered traditions and new influences.

Kulan invites me to share a meal with his extended family, stretched out beneath a stand of trees on the edge of the pasture. The blanket is overflowing with food: cakes and fruit piled in small pyramids, bread and meats; pony, caribou and moose. There are samovars and thermos flasks, wooden goblets of *kumys*, cans of Coke. I ask Kulan how the festival has changed and developed within his lifetime. 'At first, basically it was like a show,' he confides, 'but now we are becoming more aware of its essence. I'm working at it so that our people adopt a genuine approach to it.' It's hard to know how long it will take for them to rediscover, essentially reconnect with, some of their ancient traditions, while also embracing their increasingly modern way of life. 'There is real spiritual depth here,' Kulan explains, 'but only now we are beginning our journey.'

21 JUNE: BALYKTAKH

It's the dawn of the longest day. Kulan is taking me to a remote village where he says I will experience first hand the ancient Sakha connection with nature. We arrive at another break in the forest, the smoke from small fires drifts across the meadow. Small groups of people, many of them Kulan's relatives, gather at the edge of the forest, talking quietly together in the half-light. We are all waiting for the sun to come up, for a new year to begin. It's a ritual that has happened all over the world, for tens of thousands of years. These are all modern people, they could be tucked up asleep in bed or watching late-night television, but they've chosen to be here. As clouds move in from

OVERLEAF: Ceremonial shaman prayer rags tied to poles on Olkon Island, Siberia.

127

THE SHAMAN Early peoples around the world were hunter gatherers, a demanding and insecure way of life. For Arctic people, as elsewhere, the life connected to the land led to the development of polytheistic religions and creation mythologies that explained their place in nature. Such belief systems are now termed shamanism, a word derived from *saman* – the wise one – in the Tungusic language of the peoples of eastern Siberia. To the Sami he was the *noaidi*, the mediator of the shadows; to the Inuit

he was *angakkoq*, the guide who could defeat evil spirits and intercede with the gods.

The shaman was the keeper of his people's memory, the guardian of their stories and their songs. He, or she, kept the fires of tradition alight, speaking with the dead. In trances they would walk with their ancestors, flying through the realms of the spirit world. Shamans would listen to their teachings and return to pass on their message. As a healer, shamans would be called on to treat everyday illnesses and to cure deeper sickness, to animate and mend an individual's soul, or to restore the health of the tribe. In Siberia, it is said, the shaman would often drink the urine of the reindeer that had grazed on Amanita mushrooms to produce a wild cocktail of hallucinogens. Patients would then share his urine, further altering their consciousness. During ceremonies shamans would pose as different animals – perhaps taking on the vision of the falcon or the strength of the bear – dressing up in elaborate costumes and using their patterned drums to beat a hypnotic rhythm. While his earthly body entered a trance-like state, the shaman's spirit would travel to the lower reaches of the heavens.

Shamanism was viewed with fear and suspicion by Christian missionaries who came to the region following first contact between the people of the Arctic and Europeans. Siberia's 'ancient and instrinsic faith' was pronounced dead many decades ago. Collectivization, forced settlement, industrialization, and the break-up of traditional clans weakened the shaman's influence. Soviet doctrine vilified difference. The shamans were hounded, persecuted, exiled. Some were re-educated, others were shot. Those who survived disappeared into the forest. In museums you can see remnants of the past: feathered costumes, antler head-dresses, tassels and ribbons. The sacred drums now hang in showcases. Disconnected from life and the land, they are merely objects.

the north, we lift our arms, receiving the rays of the new sun in our open palms. I couldn't think of anywhere I'd rather be.

I can feel the flow of new spirituality among the Sakha. Kulan might not call himself a shaman, but there is more than an echo of this ancient religion in his work. People look to him for guidance, and he shares with them his understanding of the world. I feel a real sense of peace in his presence and I'm sorry to be leaving him, to continue on my fast journey around the Arctic. As we head on our way, he offers me some sound advice: 'Try to think less and feel more, Bruce. Do your best to ignore the endless barrage of information, try to experience the here and now, just as you and I are sitting here together.' He smiles when he sees that I agree. This is something I am searching for – what most of us wish for in the mess of our frenetic modern lives, if only we took more time to stop, to be still. 'We can feel the wind,' he continues, 'nature is all around us and it is summer. We feel alive, we can feel our heart beat.'

24 JUNE: SAKKYRYR

We are travelling north, some 800 kilometres into the Arctic Circle and the land of the midnight sun. For the next few weeks, I will live in a world of endless daylight.

ABOVE: Lunch at the *Ysyakh* festival – caribou meat and goblets of mare's milk.
OPPOSITE: A young Yakut boy in traditional dress waits for the results of the local beauty contest.
OVERLEAF: The tough Sakha horse can happily survive in the extreme conditions of Siberia's climate.

Even this remote part of the Arctic was controlled by the Soviet Union. Twenty years on from its collapse and the Sakha people who live here are returning to their roots to prosper. The Sakha horse is one of the world's toughest, specially adapted to live outdoors even in the near total dark and extreme cold of deep winter, where is can reach a deathly minus 70°C. It is able to forage for food and fend for itself. In times past, the people depended upon them for food, clothing and transportation and they are still sacred symbols of fertility and wealth. More than anything though, it was this animal that enabled the Sakha people to colonize this harsh landscape.

I'm here to meet Sergei Lukin in the remote northern town of Sakkyryr. He's one of a new generation of Sakha entrepreneurs – a breeder and dealer who manages a private herd of over a hundred semi-wild horses. He is wearing a Stetson with a Union Jack cloth badge pinned to it, perhaps for my arrival. He sports sunglasses and a long mullet, which hangs proudly like a mane over the back of his neck. He's a big talker and my opening question receives a ten-minute reply. Our translator is still smiling, but begins to look exhausted. There is one key event in the Sakha calendar that Sergei cannot afford to miss: the annual solstice races. I offer to lend my services as a stable boy for the few days I'm in town. Sergei looks me up and down, something gets lost in translation. He thinks I am offering to ride for him, so immediately calls for a horse to test me out.

ABOVE: The horses of Sakkyryr race at break-neck speeds.
OPPOSITE: Grand prize at the Sakkyryr horse racing is this handsome green machine. In Siberia, everyone wants a tractor.

BELOW: The locals have gathered to watch the races. OVERLEAF: We stop to stretch our legs and take a photograph in the warm summer sun before getting back into that wretched tank.

Up here, where the permafrost begins a metre below the surface, there is no real agriculture and animals have always provided the means of survival. Under the Soviet Union, all livestock was state owned and herding became more of a job than a way of life. Sergei generates most of his income now looking after horses for a new class of private owners from all over the area. The upcoming race will be a showcase for his skills and the strength of his business. Sergei is well on his way up the ladder, while I confront the bottom rung – simply, trying to get on one of his horses! He challenges me to a race.

Getting to the start line is proving hard enough but finally we're ready. For me, just staying on a castrated stallion bareback with only one rein is difficult, racing it is another thing altogether. No sooner have I managed to get to grips with my wild horse, careering down the valley at breakneck speed, than he decides to give me a bath and heads straight for the river. Predictably, as he jumps for the opposite bank, I'm sent flying the other way. No Sakha champion jockey am I, just a very wet TV

presenter. Victorious, Sergei helps me out of the stream. 'Well done, Bruce,' he shouts, 'you won't be racing tomorrow though as everyone would laugh too much!'

Sergei invites me to come to his house, so I can dry my clothes. We feed on pizza and vodka. He shows me the prizes he has won over the years but I get the feeling that there is more to this than just medals. Though the upcoming race will be a test of horsemanship, this summer solstice is a particularly special time for his family. His son Misha has just returned after three years in the city. He was studying for his teaching diploma and successfully graduated, but surprised them by arriving home last night. Rejecting a future in the city, he has decided to stay in the village, to teach and to help with the family firm. But, most important of all, he wants to race. Now too old, and maybe a little too heavy – though he won't admit to either – Sergei is quite literally handing over the reins to his son.

Little more than a generation ago the state would have allocated all the resources to train and support a new teacher like Misha. In the new Russia, it falls very much on entrepreneur Sergei to help him succeed. With his son back, Sergei has now got his eye on first prize and he takes me into the village to see it – a brand-new, green tractor. I joke that it's a typically Soviet sort of prize, unlike a crate of champagne, but a utilitarian object, a tool of productivity. Sergei looks at me, like I'm something of an idiot. 'Well Bruce,' he says scratching his head, 'last time we won the tractor and I sold it. I got real money, hard cash.'

26 June: Sakkyryr

It's the big day and the entire town has turned up. Sergei's son Misha, proudly wearing a white headband, leads our team in the procession. My job is simply to stay on the horse, then get well clear when the races proper begin. This series of summer races is a celebration of Sakha culture and the new spirit of enterprise. The crowds hug the starting line, drawn in the mud. Dogs scamper through our legs; money changes hands thick and fast. Contentedly full of booze, a man lies slumped against the wheels of a truck, snoring loudly. And then the races begin. Though Misha doesn't win the final big race he rides well throughout the day and the horses prove their quality. Sergei does not go home empty handed, picking up a clutch of medals and trophies doled out amid shouts and cheers from the back of a flat-bed truck. Not a tractor for Sergei this time, but he is happy to win a microwave. He may not have claimed first prize but, once again, Sergei has cemented his reputation as a respected Sakha horse breeder.

I am recognizing that there is more at stake for Sergei – in essence, the very traditions of his people – even though success has brought him the comforts of modern life. And he wants his son to share in it. He's going one better than the traditional Soviet gift. 'We couldn't just give him a new watch, could we?' Sergei jokes, as we head back into town. Instead, he tells me, they have built him a home of his own.

Misha is overwhelmed. 'I didn't expect such a present, but I'm glad of course. If I have a house, I'll have everything.'

Before I leave town, Misha gives me a tour of his new pad. Upstairs, his father has built a window so that they can look out together across the vast landscape. And that is where I am heading next, to a remote valley to meet some of the Eveny people and one of the most ubiquitous of all the Arctic animals – the reindeer.

I'm travelling up with Innokenti, a council bureaucrat with an advanced biology degree, and he's secured the use of a local 'tank'. It's actually an old Soviet armoured personnel carrier, a beastly taxi of sorts. It seems an incongruous way to travel through the land, but at least it's a vehicle that can actually manage this vast boggy terrain. It's a new acquisition and the drivers are still getting to grips with it. They were evidently ripped off; it was an awful machine. There must be other vehicles that could travel this way without churning up the terrain, belching out exhaust fumes and destroying tree and permafrost alike. As we claw our way over hills, through forests and across streams, it's a numbing, deafening experience. We're riding to the end of the earth in a tumble dryer.

As much as possible we all try to sit on top of the vehicle, the seats above the cab being the favourite spots, central and on the roof seemed to be the place of least movement. I tried to persuade Gavin to let me ride by horse to the camp because that is the way I would have gone if I was alone, but as we had so much gear, he wanted to make a feature of this tracked vehicle tearing through the summer landscape, and I guess he was right in a way.

We tried doing some filming on the first day but it was almost impossible. We're really struggling with the big camera. Gavin hates it more than I do and the film is suffering as a result. It's just too unwieldy and we can't do half the shots we would normally get, and it's such a shame that for the sake of extra pixels and clarity we can't get half the intimacy that comes with the speed, proximity and manipulation of a smaller camera. Gavin simply can't film on a horse and struggles in the rumbling tank too. When it comes to me being on a horse or reindeer later in the programme, the intimacy and authenticity will suffer I'm sure, as the crew won't be able to ride alongside me. Overnight we camped at a log cabin in the woods. The engine is off. At last, silence.

The following morning, we're all a little battered and bruised and reluctant to get back in the rust bucket. But on we must go. After a few more miles following a branch in the river, we are rewarded by a wide valley with a forest of larch and willow, deep green meadows, dwarf birch, and flowers of all colours: snap dragons, forget-me-nots, buttercups and daisies. Rarely have I seen anything as beautiful as this carpet of flowers, backlit by the low sun – but never have I heard anything as ugly as this dreadful machine, tearing through the turf, grinding in my head. At last a moment's peace – we stop by the riverbank to drink vodka in honour of a shaman, or wise man, who once lived here. A moment for reflection, then it's back in the beast.

Thankfully, before long, another moment of quiet – one of the tank's wheels has come away from its track. We halt to fix it, but it snaps almost immediately. I feel a rush of pleasure, perhaps we might be able to ditch this thing and head off on horseback? The nearest village is a day away, and in the other direction from where we want to go. Perhaps, says Innokenti vaguely, sensing my unrest, there might be another village 250 miles or so beyond the nearest hills. Yet, amazingly, within twenty minutes of hammering and Russian swearing, the track is fixed, the tank fires up its engine and we are off once more. Living out here you've got to be pretty resourceful – make a fire, ride a horse, fix a tank. I try to write some more notes in my journal, but the noise saps my will to create or to find some peace to think.

Weeks later I'm shown some lines by Fyodor Tyutchev, a poet who'd followed the mighty Pushkin to become one of Russia's finest:

Russia cannot be understood with the mind,
Or measured by ordinary measure:
She stands alone, unique –
In Russia, one can only believe.

This amuses me now as I recall those days trapped in that infernal tin can, not understanding why, or indeed how, we would continue on our journey. Foreigners find so much that is unfathomable in Russia. It's often best not to ask why, to worry or to question, but just to get on with whatever it is you are trying to do. Maybe Siberia was testing me; I had to stop being so soft and just give in to it, to accept some tiny discomfort and to trust in my companions. Head down, eyes closed, I retreat into my thoughts.

30 JUNE: DELONG VALLEY

After just two more days of bone-crunching imprisonment, we finally reach a remote valley where I'm hoping to join an encampment of Eveny herders. These are the foothills of the Verkhoyansk Mountains and the range stretches for over 1,000 kilo-

OPPOSITE ABOVE: During the summer months the herders' camp is full of children who come to help out and learn a little more about the Eveny way of life.
OPPOSITE BELOW: The tank pulls up by the river bed. With the peace and quiet we take our chance to get some sleep in our tent.

metres, rising in an arc east of the Lena River right to the shores of the Arctic Ocean. These valleys are the coldest inhabited places in the world, sometimes as low as minus 70°C in the depths of the Russian winter. In the summer, temperatures soar into the forties. They are home to the Eveny people.

These people are reindeer herders, who for millennia have inhabited this extreme landscape. There are fewer than 20,000 Eveny today. After the fall of the Soviet Union in the 1990s, the herds almost totally collapsed. I'm here to find out how one group has fought back from the brink of extinction and with it saved a unique way of life.

This is Brigade 8, a small group of men who follow the herd throughout the year. I'm here at the busiest time of year, the count, when the herders discover the exact number of new calves born. Almost half the herd is owned by the state, the rest to fortunate individuals and prosperous families. Every newborn calf born to privately owned mothers must be earmarked before the corral deadline, otherwise it becomes government property. I'm welcomed into a tent, and to the first of many glasses of vodka. I've brought a bottle with me and offer it to the table as a gift. A murmur of approval, and it's opened immediately. The hospitality, as always, is warm, with bowls of reindeer meat, fish (salted and raw), unleavened bread, pound cake and other sugared treats. It's traditional for new arrivals to feed the fire in thanks for a safe journey. I do it with vodka, which gives a satisfying whoosh. We hope for success in the weeks ahead.

These men work shifts around the clock while there is 24-hour daylight. The reindeer need to feed continuously at this time of year so they can put on enough weight and make it through the long, dark winter. Some of the deer look like a bunch of scruffy teenagers, mostly because they are in the middle of moulting their heavy winter coats, but apparently they are all in pretty good nick. Their antlers are quite large and covered in the beautiful thick velvet fur that coats them as they continue to grow. They will reach maturity in a few weeks, eventually harden and the velvet moults. The male antlers fall off after the rut and the females lose theirs as winter turns to spring.

Despite only just arriving, it appears that tomorrow we will move on to new pastures some distance further up the valley. The specially trained riding reindeer that will also pull our sledges are called the *uchakh*. We need to catch thirty of these strong, adult males. I follow camp leader Vasili, who has agreed to show me how it's done. Vasili is a man of huge experience. He's been with the herd for over forty years, and grew up with it rather than going to school, through the good times and the bad. He's now so hard of hearing that his elder brother follows him at every step, repeating everything asked of him in a loud voice, herding him around the camp. They make an interesting pair. He teaches me the basics of lassoing. In all, after some effort, I catch about four animals, though only two are the right ones. I spend much more time being dragged through puddles of reindeer shit and helping to wrestle others to the ground, as we try to hold them steady while their ears are cut for marking. The special *uchakh* usually have parts of their antlers removed for safety, but as I go to catch one

THESE PAGES: Some of the Eveny reindeer herders who became our friends.

ABOVE: Two of the *uchakh* – the trained reindeer – are saddled up, as we prepare for the migration.

OPPOSITE: Vasili leads the train of *uchakh* reindeer as we move up the valley.

animal, an antler breaks. The Eveny have an unusual way of cleaning the injury and preventing infection. We cut the antler straight, suck the wound and the bleeding stops almost immediately.

1 JULY: DELONG VALLEY

It's the day of the migration and the entire camp is packing up. During the summer months the camp is full of school children who come here to earn money and discover more about the traditional Eveny way of life. The kids work really hard and say they enjoy it. A young girl saunters past on the back of a reindeer, casually listening to her iPod. There's a lot to learn though. Under the old regime, the herds became the property of the state and the Eveny were forced to send their children to school and give up a truly nomadic way of life. With the collapse of Communism, many of the brigades failed to survive the transition to private ownership. The way of life is now seen as something of a national treasure, yet only with some subsidy from the profits of the region's diamond mines are the herds growing once more. Few of the herders have children though, most are ageing bachelors. I'm told the Soviet ideology broke many

of the tribal families, the children attended residential schools and their mothers returned to be with them in the nearby villages. The nomadic family unit is a thing of the past here, but there is so much knowledge that can be gained from the land. I wonder who is going to take over this life when these men are too old to work? I fear I know the answer.

After a night of powerful dreams, I want to ask more questions about the spiritual connections to the land. I speak with our fixer Innokenti, keeper of the tank, and he does little to hide his contempt for the neo-shamans in the city. New age philosophies mean nothing to him. He doesn't much care for the likes of Kulan. He is a product of a system and although he's outwardly nice he harbours entrenched opinions about many things. I try to explain my feelings for appreciating all manner of belief systems, but the words don't always come out right. Our translator is again working hard to keep up. Innokenti doesn't see the link between alternative medicine, neo-shamanism and the shamans of old. And he doesn't seem to like those who don't fit his opinion of what his people should be doing. He is a clever man, a scientist after all, but his analytical mind seems somewhat at odds with the locals who are very gentle and noticeably become quiet when he talks for them. This frustrates me when I want to explore their feelings more.

We set off, a motley caravan of herders and film crew, dragging our sledges over grass and bare earth, through some of the most extraordinary scenery. We enter another wide glaciated valley, beautiful green mountains crowning our route. Snowy peaks lie off to the south and once on the hoof everything calms down. I tried to clear my mind and feel my senses as Kulan had instructed me. After more than an hour of silence, I feel more alive, my senses sharp. I asked for confirmation of my dreams and hopes and it was given to me by this wave of happiness. This powerful moment doubled my experience of the journey. I was in bliss.

The deer are easy to ride. We all had sticks to aid with balance but they weren't needed at the pace we were going, even with the unsteady sensation of riding atop the front legs of the animal. Mongolian herders ride the spine, sitting in the centre on the back, which would undoubtedly be a much smoother ride, but they don't live long as it puts so much pressure on the back bone.

Many of the herders are still too shy to approach the crew and they refuse to stop for the cameras. They move among each other, working without a sound, intuitively.

Their disregard for the spoken word is noticeable. I have passed a few of them on some errand and they have remained silent despite my efforts to say hello. It's not hostile, just that idle talk to them is unnecessary. I'm aware that filling the silence with empty words may well be an expression of social insecurity but to me this sort of exchange is more like a cultural pleasantry. Perhaps I am wrong? I can't wait to ignore someone back home when they say hi when I've already seen them that day. Maybe the Eveny are right and silence is better. I will give it a go. Certainly we are culturally prone to filling silence with talk. Gavin is an expert at making noise and Sarah, our assistant on this trip, constantly chatters to herself. Today she even asked me if I was meditating.

One of the herders I'm getting on best with is Yegor. He's in his forties but only joined the brigade a year ago. As a child he was brought up in a herding community, and after troubles in the village he has decided to return to the herding life. I'm helping him set up camp, at the head of the valley. I ask him about the surrounding hills. Someone told me that the reason they face the tents up the valley in this way is because of spirits in the land. 'No,' he says quite simply, bursting my romance, 'it's because the wind blows from over there.' We laugh. 'I'm a modern person Bruce, I don't know if it's spirits or not. For me it's all about the wind!'

OPPOSITE: One of the special new calves is comforted after its ear has been cut, marking it for the tally. There are few white reindeer here now. The Soviets apparently got rid of so many, saying they were too bourgeois, too unique for the herd.
BELOW: A reindeer is milked in time for breakfast.

I've noticed with my questions, such as this, that people are very quick to deny any of the old spiritual beliefs. It's as if they're ashamed of them, which is no surprise after the Soviet quashing and the ascendancy of modern science. But I wonder if offering my own perspective may soften the question. 'To me the hills talk, what about you?' I ask. This does the trick and he tells me that yes, indeed, the landscape is alive to him.

Managing the reindeer at this time of year is all about the plague of mosquitoes that descend on the herd. Left to their own devices the animals would run into the wind to try and shake off these parasites. If there is no wind, they group tightly together, reducing their overall surface area. You can escape the mosquitoes on windy ridges, because the insects can't compete with even a moderate breeze, or on patches of snow where the air is cooler and insect activity is reduced. As a traveller, it's a good lesson to learn if you don't want to be constantly eaten alive.

I'm heading out with Piotr, one of the most experienced of the new generation of herders, on my first evening shift. Even though it looks like a sea of legs and antlers to me, Piotr is able to recognize every single one of these adult reindeer in a herd of almost 2,000. He's one of the few men here who can do this. Our job will be to guide them to the best pasture with the fewest insects so that the reindeer can gain the most weight in this short summer season. At night, when it's cooler, they take to the hills to feast upon lichen.

I have been with the Eveny for a week now and I'm getting used to a diet of reindeer meat and bread. There is always something on the table as we are working in shifts around the clock. In a week from now we'll know how much the herd has grown in the past few years. Yegor has got a day off and I get a feeling he's not the sort

of guy to sit around. He calls me over. 'Let's climb that mountain, Bruce, it'll be fun.' I think he wants me to join him on a leisurely hike, so I happily agree and we shake on it. Immediately, many of the guys in camp are placing bets on who'll reach the top first. Yegor had actually challenged me to race him – another thing that got lost in translation – and I'd accepted so there's no backing out now.

Yegor finds it all hilarious. The other guys are lining up with binoculars, ready for the big race. 'Get your glasses boys,' he calls to them, 'when I get to the top you'll all be able to see when I take a pee. It's a problem being 40 you know!' 'Don't piss into the wind,' someone else shouts at me, as I walk to join Yegor, doing his stretches and ready to go. Though I've been all over the Arctic these past few months, I'm fat after too much time in hotels and on flights, and I've never felt so unfit. I run through all the usual excuses in my head. A quick look at one another and then we're off. Yegor doesn't look back. I don't see his face again until I clamber up to the summit, a good few hours later, and he's there, fresh as a daisy, smiling at me, urging me to the top.

Yegor has won the race, but maybe there is another reason why he's got me up here. The view is magnificent; no mosquitoes, a fresh breeze, the reindeer herd just stamp-sized on the valley floor below us and mountains as far as the eye can see. 'There is some power here,' he says, 'I can feel it in the nature here. Maybe, yes, perhaps it is the spirits in the land Bruce. It's hard for me to explain, so I wanted to share it with you.' I'm delighted he dragged me up the mountain.

The morning after, it's back to work. I spend some time deer-milking, which is not as easy as you might think, and certainly more tricky than cows, horses and goats, which I have tried my hand at in the past. Three hours later and just one mug of musty milk. Today I'm going to take part in breaking in a new *uchakh*, one of the

THESE PAGES: The reindeer showed Innokenti who's boss.

riding reindeer. The process takes several weeks, and for the male we have just found it is day one. It might look a little unkind, but by becoming a *uchakh* this reindeer has a long life ahead of him. But if I try to ride him more, I'm unlikely to last much longer. After five attempts, and five falls, I accept I'm not the man for the job. The whole camp was in hysterics and I was bruised to hell. I received laughs and thumbs up from many people, including the old leader Vasili. After me a couple of others had a go. Innokenti stepped up first, which was good of him, but he didn't last long either and left it at one attempt.

On his first try Piotr stays on for some time, but Yegor, who was helping him, let go of the tether so when Piotr was thrown, an inevitability at this stage, the animal broke loose. It ran off to join the herd, still wearing its saddle. We eventually managed to find him and Piotr had another go, managing to sit on long enough to ride out the worst of the bucks and tossings. 'It takes many weeks to break one in,' Piotr explains. 'We start gently on the first day and then leave him to recover. In three days we can

start with the training again. Over time, we begin to understand each other.' Piotr has the strength and the patience for this work. It is no surprise to me that he is fast becoming the leader of this band.

We slaughtered another deer this evening; it took longer than ever to locate one, because they only knew of one animal that fitted the bill – a calf-less mother, fat to eat and of certain ownership. Piotr did the dispatching, lightning fast as ever. A sharp knife to the back of the head, one stab in behind the brain, then a wooden plug to stop the bleeding. Dead instantly, the animal was butchered roughly for the pot. The butchery here is very different to Canada, where the meat never touched the ground and no bones were broken and sinew and ligaments were split elegantly to separate the joints. I suppose everyone has their own style. Not worse, just different.

During the summer months, the herders like to supplement their diet of reindeer. I'm heading off with a few guys from the camp to a nearby lake. The nets were set overnight and we quickly pull in a dozen fish for the pot. It's not only their skill in this

THIS PAGE: Training these reindeer requires huge skill and patience – perhaps not so easy with a film crew following you around.

environment that impresses me, but the very closeness of their relationship to nature. It's almost like they are in a dialogue with it, talking, thanking it, aware of its presence and respectful of the way the land provides for them. By the lake, in an informal ceremony, we sink a glass of vodka in its honour, offer a cigarette and say some words of thanks. We laugh a little, then head back to camp to escape the biting insects as the evening draws in. There is a richness and kinship in this land, however bleak it looks.

Yet always the infernal mosquitoes! Nothing but a good breeze keeps these little blighters down. They mock me when I, naively, first thought of using repellent. They laugh at bug spray, they work their way around the thick smoke of our fires to seek out any weak spot. Much of the time our crew wore special anti-mosquito hats, the *nakomarnik*, looking like beekeepers armed for a fight. In past times here, indigenous people wove swathes of fine netting with the long hairs of a horse's tail. I'd read somewhere that members of the Tungus tribe would carry smoke pots with them wherever they went. The Voguls retreated into smoke-filled huts for most of the summer, only emerging to begin their hunting and travelling as winter approached. In the modern Arctic, these little insects are as inventive and persistent as ever. Some would ping around in my ears, crash into my eyes, maybe taking a chance to surf down into my throat. They'd creep into the tents at night and encircle us, whining, swooping, driving grown men to madness. It's good training in the art of Zen, I can tell you. My new abilities to control my mind and try to be calm allows me to laugh at these little blighters, whereas a previous me would certainly have gone insane. The pages of my journal are lined with squashed mosquitoes that have strayed too close. As I lie asleep at night I imagine the whole valley is humming as these tiny monsters mass in their billions.

6 July: Delong Valley

This morning I rode out with the herd on a newly trained *uchakh*. The animal was not happy at all when I sat on him and after a second or two of trying to rid itself of me decided to sit down, literally flat on the ground. A form of conscientious objection maybe – how cool. I was ushered onto another one which was also half trained. This fellow was equally resilient but hadn't cottoned on to the sit-it-out form of protest so was gradually won over to come on a jaunt with me. I fell off him a few times, but only on saddling up, never when moving which I was pleased with. Sometimes his back legs or forelegs gave way completely and we fell together, me still astride his back. Once this was because the saddle was too far back, but mostly because he just wasn't used to the weight.

Last night I headed out with Piotr to join the kids on the night shift. I was still sore, bruised and physically fatigued in all the muscles I needed to stay balanced on a saddle. As a result it wasn't as blissful as I'd hoped. Add to that the billions of mosquitoes in my nose, eyes and mouth, it was no romantic dream. The route we pushed the animals along was tough, up and over steep slopes from one valley to the next, through streams, broad dry stony riverbeds, deep bogs and marshes and across stunning meadows, full of more fantastic flowers. I enjoyed it and felt the gratitude that I should feel for such an experience, but it could easily have gone the other way. I was tired and fell a number of times, especially mounting and dismounting. I was lucky to have some quieter moments with Piotr, away from the big camera, so asked him a little more about hunting, his family life, and the cultural future for his people. He believes that you don't need a shaman to be able to commune with, or believe in, the spirit world. He said that, in a way, we are all shaman. I agree with this. He thought the land was alive, some places being especially powerful. Most herders can't articulate this or won't do so because they are embarrassed to be seen as backward by outsiders. For others, Piotr explained, it was surely enough that they live it, though can't quite express it. I was so pleased to hear his thoughts as it made every reindeer bruise worthwhile.

It's the final tally after several weeks of earmarking. Council official Innokenti checks the record of each private owner together with the number of new calves born. It's also a chance for the herders to find out how much their personal fortune has grown in this post-Soviet Russia. We have recorded over 300 new calves born to private deer, most with different owners. Vasili though has almost forty new calves, a considerable number which makes him a rich man in relative terms. Piotr has eleven, poor Yegor no deer at all. I feel for him and even if he were to own one deer, a female, it would take many years for him to accumulate any wealth, even if he had no bad luck from wolves, health, ice, or other problems. It's a tough restart for him.

Of the private calves born there are forty-seven owners, most of whom are not herders and so a very intricate system of reciprocity is in place to pay individual herders

OPPOSITE: Camp life on a rare moment when the mosquitoes were not about.

or the collective brigade to look after their numbers. There is no way of actually calcu-
lating what each payment is as each deal is different and private. I'd been told that gifts
or items such as a saddle, horses, firewood and food being placed in locations were
typical forms of transaction. I'd even heard mention of a payment being an introduction
to a man who is worth knowing because he works for the local authority accounting
department. How exactly one saddle can pay a whole group of herders is a mystery to
me, even now. Some deals are done with individual herders, even though the whole
team are involved in working to look after the herd. This form of trade predates money
and reinforces social bonds. It works but there are, no doubt, problems and confusion.

   It's my final day with the herders and I'm going out on a full nightshift with
Yegor. Though we've now spent much time together, I know so little about him.
Yegor was brought up an Eveny herder but only returned to this way of life two years

ABOVE: The reindeer are grouped ready for milking. They look like a bunch of scruffy teenagers.

ago. I was wondering where he had been in the dark years following the collapse of the Soviet Union, when the herders teetered on the brink of extinction.

'I don't know how to explain it you,' he says, as we rest in the lee of a hill. 'I have a problem with drink, I got separated from my children. It's scary when you're left alone. If I'd stayed a herder back then, now I would have many reindeer by now. I'm having to start all over again.' We stop for a while on the hillside, sometimes sharing stories with each other, or simply sitting together in silence, listening to the falling rain. 'There is light,' he says, after some time, 'there are positive changes. Now I'm allowed to see my children but I must carry on working as a reindeer herder … otherwise they'll be upset in the Otherworld. My grandfather is there.'

Yegor, who had so roundly beaten me on the mountain, was now challenging my perception of the indigenous people of the Arctic. I've always admired these traditional

BELOW: Newly born reindeer are marked in the tally book, using an intricate system of ownership and responsibility. Its symbols and patterns are a puzzle to me.

OPPOSITE: Yegor and I talk about the future, sitting with our reindeer in the evening drizzle.

ways of life. In reality, what I now see around me is not the past but the future. Supporting the Eveny way of life is, simply put, good modern social policy. It's a mixture of the nomadic and the act of being settled, settling oneself in mind, that will bring most success. One's view changes. Instead of looking back, or looking too far into the future, one begins to move toward a genuine feeling of responsibility to what is local, to the positive aspects of the land that is their home. It's the Eveny skill with reindeer and their intimacy with nature that enables them to be productive, to have balance, to feel connection in their lives. Once that link is broken, the consequences are often catastrophic. And perhaps it is this relationship with wild nature that also answers my personal journey.

It's time for me to leave the Eveny and head home. As we begin packing our camp, Yegor and Piotr come to find me and give me a gift. It's not something I can take home, to keep in a box or display on my mantelpiece, but it's something greater than anything I have ever brought back from my travels. 'We've named that mountain "Bruce". We'll look at it every year and think of you. Maybe even laugh a little…' It's a simple and genuine gesture, not a joke at my expense. I am touched to tears. I have no way to respond, but to thank them with all my heart.

The spiritual revival that I saw on the beginning of my journey in Siberia is not, at first sight, present here and initially I was a little bemused, maybe even disappointed

at having come to a place where the word shaman arose. I suppose I expected a more obvious spirituality, ceremonies, rituals, dancing medicine men and all manner of new lessons to be learned. But the Soviets got rid of all the shamans, there seem to be none left, in the old sense at least. The interesting thing, deep in the mountains, is that in some ways there's no need for a revival here. The herders are so in tune and aware of their animals and their landscape that the spirit world, which the shamans were only ever a pathway to anyway, is as alive today as it has ever been.

Shamanism is perhaps the oldest form of spirituality. The belief in an animated world where the sky, the mountains and the rivers were alive with spirits naturally meant that we humans needed to respect the land. Not to do so would bring trouble. As a young man I was told that animism was backward, full of fear and bogus ritual. It makes me very sad to know that this view is still commonly held. All this must change, as surely there are real lessons for us here in this sensitive way of approaching our world. If modern spirituality is about simple gestures, about listening to others and looking to nature for guidance, for support, and inspiration, then – no matter how extreme this environment, no matter how cold it gets in the winter – there is a beating heart here. As long as the link between man and nature is left unbroken, or rather as long as man is willing to listen to nature, then there may be hope for all of us.

FOLLOWING PAGES: A Russian expedition tank crossing the Arctic ice.

RUSSIA'S ARCTIC FRONTIER

Despite a recent wave of Russian diplomacy, many fear the Arctic will become a battleground for control of the massive reserves of oil and gas thought to lie under the Arctic Ocean. The largest 'Arctic state' geographically and a major player in the global energy marketplace, Russia now commands a central role in the international politics of the North. Polar geopolitics have thus become a hot topic as our demand for energy shows no sign of abating. Some see this new era as the perfect moment for the region to become a 'Pole of Peace', calling for polar multi-lateralism of the like not seen since the signing of the Antarctic Treaty, some fifty years ago.

In the grimy shipyards of St Petersburg, the hulks of newly painted red metal give us an obvious signal of Russian ambitions. The strange construction – part ship, part industrial site – when completed in 2012 will be the first of eight floating nuclear power stations which the present government wants to place along Russia's northern coast. Each costs some $400 million to create and, it is claimed, could supply electricity and heating for new communities of up to 45,000 people. An enhanced fleet of nuclear submarines will also continue their patrols under the sea ice as securitization of the region increases. Providing a reliable energy supply, these sites would then enable the exploration of the sea floor, fuelling further vessels and facilities and the setting up of drilling platforms to extract oil and gas.

Moscow is claiming more than a million square kilometres of extra territory in the Arctic, stretching from its current borders, just offshore, all the way to the North Pole itself. This disputed territory includes an underwater

mountain called the Lomonosov ridge, a geological feature that some Russian scientists claim could hold as much as 75 billion barrels of oil – a figure greatly exceeding the country's already vast and proven reserves. The government has declared that the Arctic should be Russia's main source of oil and gas by 2020, in the face of claims from other nations.

As Russia continues to build the infrastructure needed to operate in the Arctic, its explorers have also announced efforts to provide the scientific evidence needed to convince the United Nations that Russia's claim to the Lomonosov ridge is valid. Flamboyant adventurer Artur Chilingarov, who in 2007 used a mini-submarine to plant a titanium Russian flag on the seabed at the Pole, has just launched a new expedition – a research station drifting on an ice floe, manned by

fifteen Russian scientists – which plans to undertake seismic surveys and collect soil samples from the ocean floor. 'Regardless of climate change, no matter whether it is getting warmer or colder,' he announced, 'nothing changes for these people: They live and work on ice for almost a year without their families and in extreme conditions – they are true heroes.'

Unsurprisingly, many are alarmed by this sudden increase in activity. International governments are welcoming the new dialogue but watching each development carefully. Environmental groups have been quick to voice their concerns, warning of the catastrophic consequences of a nuclear accident in the fragile Arctic environment, not to mention the difficulties and risks inherent in extracting resources in such extreme conditions.

ALASKA

Alaska
THE GOLD ISN'T ALL

'People will always have different opinions, I can't stop that, but for us this whale is a blessing. It's what we look forward to each and every year and it's what we teach our children. It's a chance for us to celebrate our food and be thankful. When was the last time you did that?'

Alaska. It's America's last great wilderness and the frontier spirit is still strong. It's a land of vast natural wealth and fortunes to be made. For hundreds of years, pioneers have headed north from the rest of the country's states, the so-called lower forty-eight, in search of adventure and a new future. The sea still teems with fish and the rivers wash gold from the mountains. In the Far North, there are huge reserves of oil and gas and Alaska is set to become the next frontier for offshore hydrocarbon exploration. This is a land where the American Dream can come true, for better or worse.

This landscape has sustained the Inupiat people for thousands of years but now their traditional way of life is at odds with modern sensibilities. At one of the places I'm intending to travel, the remote village of Kaktovik, outsiders are not always welcome. The people have been badly represented by southern journalists and film-makers in the past, their ways misunderstood. The people are cautious, wary, and it will take time and honesty before a few of the community are willing to let me into their lives. Killing whales may seem barbaric, but it's the lifeblood of this culture and part of an ancient Alaskan tradition of harvesting the wealth of the seas. I wonder what I will make of it?

THIS PAGE: Alaska, the biggest, brashest, boldest and most beautiful of all American states. The cool waters of Prince William Sound are rich in salmon at this time of year.

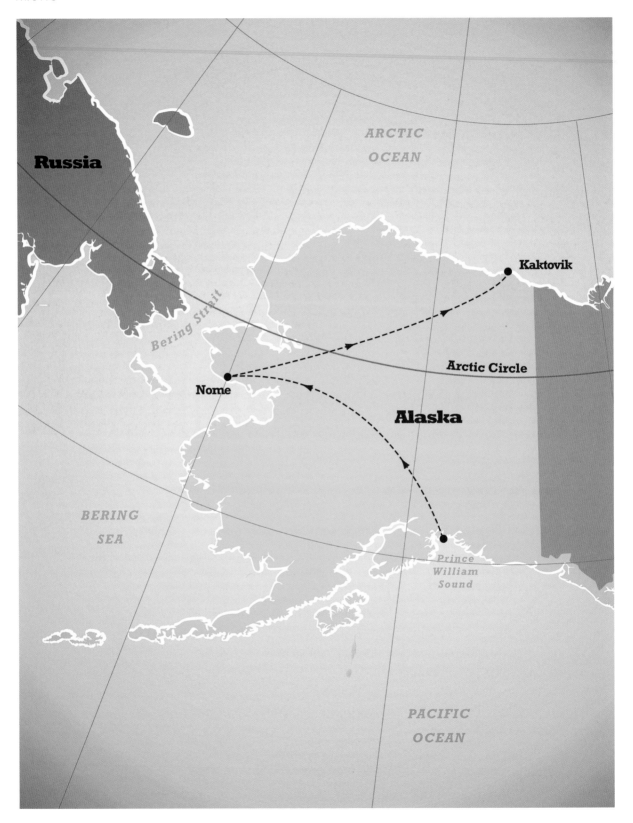

21 AUGUST: PRINCE WILLIAM SOUND

Our film begins on a small boat, chugging along in sheets of rain, as we weave our way through a maze of islands in the cool waters of southern Alaska's Prince William Sound. I'm here at that magical time when the salmon are preparing to run the gauntlet to reach their spawning grounds. Every year it happens and every year the predators line up to take part in a feeding frenzy. Those who take the lion's share, of course, are the fishermen who are out here for the salmon season, catching tens of thousands of fish a day. I've come to meet fisherman Tim Cabana, and his wife Berry, who spend three or four months out on the boat every summer. They have two deck-hands, Russell and Butch, and also on the crew are the Cabanas' children, 19-year-old Kami and 17-year-old Tanner.

Work on board the trawler stops for no one, and within minutes of my arrival the Cabanas are immediately busy setting the nets for the next catch. Everyone on the crew has a specific job, and at first I'm not quite sure what to do, but before I can get stuck in I need to get kitted out. The small deck is a slippery, busy place with lots of equipment moving around, and it's clear I've got a lot to learn.

ABOVE: I'm here to join the fishermen making a fortune from the annual salmon run. Two purse-seine fishing boats work in tandem to follow the flow of fish making for the rivers to spawn.

Salmon fishing in Alaska is extremely profitable. The mature fish aggregate here in huge numbers every year before they swim up rivers and streams to spawn and then die. Though salmon population levels are of concern in the Atlantic, in Alaska stocks are still abundant. Tim's boat alone catches about 30,000 pounds in weight of fish a day, which is worth roughly $12,000. And they fish for a hundred days in a row until the end of the salmon run. All the crew receive a healthy share of the profits. Even young Tanner, who should be at school, is earning serious pocket money. He's on about a thousand bucks a day, which his Dad is investing for him. 'So he doesn't just waste it all on parties with his friends,' Tim shouts across the deck. He has just bought his son an apartment in Hawaii. For the remainder of the year, the Cabanas live in a ski resort. So when they're not fishing, or soaking up the rays on the beach in Maui, they're on the slopes.

Tim has three brothers out here, all operating their own boats. The business was started by their father who came to Alaska from Indiana during the post-war depression to try to make his fortune. Now aged 83, Tim's father Roy still insists on coming

out to sea. He's still the king of this family affair. At the end of each day, the tender boat turns up to take away the catch. The Alaskan salmon business is worth some $11 billion a year and employs 10 per cent of the population here. These fish will be gutted, packed in ice and shipped out, with almost half of them going to markets in Japan, the rest to the USA and Europe. This time of year they're catching mainly pinks and a few silvers, just two of the five different Pacific salmon species. The salmon are leaving the ocean in the millions, heading up through the Gulf of Alaska towards their spawning grounds in the hundreds of rivers and tributaries all along the coast. When they are caught, the fish are sucked up from the hold with a vacuum pump, weighed, and then shipped back to port by a tender. It means that we can stay out during the night, to fish again early tomorrow at first light. The cycle continues.

I've had a great night's sleep, and I'm ready for a hard day's work. We're on our way to the next fishing ground, and I feel a great sense of freedom out here. You could say the Cabanas are living the American Dream, working hard and making a good honest living from the bounty of the sea. Over hot coffee at the wheel in the bridge,

as the sun comes up over the mountains, Tim describes to me the pull of the land. 'Of course as I grew up here with my Dad, it was a way of making a living. But, you know, as my kids and my brothers have been involved all the way along, it really has become a way of life for us.' After almost fifty years of fishing in these waters the Cabanas have worked out the seasonal cycles and migration patterns of the different species of salmon. Up in the crow's nest Tim keeps a good eye on the water to see which way the fish are heading and looks for the best place to put out the net.

This type of fishing is called purse-seining, ideal for fish that school in groups close to the surface or the shore. Sardines and mackerel, herring and anchovies are also gathered in this way the world over. It's apparently the least stressful way of catching fish in these large numbers; they are not snagged or damaged before they are brought aboard. The long net is drawn out behind the boat across the channel, with the top edge lined with floats, keeping it at the surface. The bottom edge of this fine netting sinks to form a huge underwater curtain. We wait about 20 minutes until a significant number has been stopped by the net, and then one end of the net is pulled around by another small boat, a skiff, corralling all the fish inside. To stop the fish escaping and to get them on board, the bottom of the net is drawn in by the line creating one enclosed bowl of netting, rather like a purse. The catch is hauled aboard in a flurry of scales and slime, and unceremoniously poured into a hold where the fish will die from lack of oxygen and be chilled to just above freezing. The crew grab their meals while they can, before they're back on deck ready for the next set.

The Cabana family are very at home in Alaska and see it as a land of golden opportunities. It was this way when Tim's father Roy came here in the 1950s, and though it's in every sense a modern state – a nation in itself – the frontier spirit is still very much alive. 'Bruce, there's over 600,000 square miles in this state, about a square mile for every person. This is big country. The potential of this place hasn't really been touched, there's just so much space, not enough time.' As if perfectly on queue, we're interrupted by a command on the radio. It's our turn to set the nets. Talk over: it's time to get back to work. Tim and his brothers fish together in what's known as a wolf pack, taking it in turns to 'hunt their prey'. While one is circling the catch, the next boat has already set out its net, and the third is waiting to go next. Working in such a way means that almost every fish in a particular place is caught. Few will escape, and it is only the restrictions on the working day that allow others to reach the spawning grounds.

In some ways I'm annoyed at myself for not delving deeper into the story. One question I wished I'd asked them directly was whether or not the millions of fish represented life or just simply money? I think I'd know the answer but I have let myself down by not exploring this on camera. Something, somewhere just didn't quite feel right to me. After all the talk, I get a sense these fish are just a commodity. This family are not bad people, quite the opposite, but my stay here makes me ques-

OPPOSITE: Once the small skiff tender boat has set the net, the ends are brought round and pulled up together, as if a purse. In the flurry of activity, hundreds, sometimes thousands, of fish are brought onboard in one go. I try my best to look the part and not slip up.
OVERLEAF: Prince William Sound is a beautiful, sheltered body of water on the eastern side of the Kenai Peninsula. crowned by the snow-covered peaks of the Chugach Mountains.

tion whether we are respecting the natural world enough. As always, I feel a hyp-ocrite, part of the problem: I enjoy eating fish and, likewise, I'm lucky enough to fly all over the world for a living. I benefit from being able to travel in this way. I know that I'm also guilty of not respecting the natural world consistently, no matter how much I might worry about it, or try to do my best. I promise myself to listen more without judgement, to spend my time here happily and take it for what it is. Opin-ions can come later.

24 AUGUST: PRINCE WILLIAM SOUND

I'm back on the cork floats again, and this time I'm determined to get it right. Stack-ing the corks is actually much harder than it looks and after wrestling with the net on the shifting deck, getting hollered at by Tim and teased by the crew, I know I've made another mess of it. For the next set I'm out in the skiff with Tanner. From here I'm in the perfect spot to see whether my corks go out properly. So far so good. I'm relieved to see there's been no problems, but Kami is back on the case and is doing it with con-summate ease. The Cabanas certainly have a unique lifestyle and they tell me they wouldn't swap it for anything. But bringing up children on a fishing boat hasn't always been easy. 'All the kids have been raised on the boat,' mum Berry tells me, as I rejoin them later to help pull in the catch. 'Seriously, I'd be breast-feeding with a kid in one hand, maybe grabbing the wheel with the other. Or I'd rush from the helm, out to help with the nets, then rush back inside the cabin to deal with a screaming baby. And you have to teach them how to learn to swim real early,' she smiles when remembering – the good old days, she says – but I suppose these things always improve with time. It must have been a nightmare for the young mother, but it was her choice and they survived it. And now they are leading the business here.

The wild salmon run in Alaskan waters is one of the greatest on Earth and it is also one of the best managed. The Alaska Department of Fish and Game have an intricate system of fisheries governance. The Board of Fisheries has eighty-two public advisory councils across the state, which gather in proposals from industry, indigenous groups and the public. All Alaska salmon species and commercial operations have to be certi-fied by the Marine Stewardship Council, in stark contrast to the Russian fisheries across the Bering Strait and along the Kamchatka Peninsula. Much has been achieved here in Alaska, but obviously much remains to be done. Alaskans went from federally controlled salmon management in the 1940s to local management after statehood was granted in 1959. At the turn of the millennium, Alaska took the proactive leap forward when all salmon operations were to be MSC certified. At present levels the fishery here is in good shape – the profits are huge, and the stocks remain in balance.

The trawlers have to stop fishing at night to allow the salmon respite to reach their spawning grounds. But as dawn breaks it's back to business. With thirty-three

OPPOSITE: On the corks again. Sometimes I'm really crap at a job and this was one of them. I never quite mastered it. Thanks for the orange gloves guys!

hatcheries across Alaska producing two billion fish a year, this is a highly lucrative industry – the future looks good for the Cabana family as long as water quality is maintained. I'm not sure, but wonder what releasing so many hatchlings does to an already fragile and not completely know ecosystem.

The brothers have netted about $2 million worth this season, so I can see why they're happy. It takes a huge amount of skill though; it's hard work and money well earned. 'It's not brain science to catch them Bruce, you know, you've just gotta be a little bit smarter than a fish, that's all.' Tim's modesty belies a lifetime's experience. It's bravado too, but he is sensitive, respectful of what he is doing here. The fishery is healthy as a result of this attitude, despite the huge volume of fish they are able to catch. Tim accepts that elsewhere there are really negative opinions about over-fishing, about industrial operations that have emptied parts of our oceans where some fish populations will never recover. I think of the collapse of the Northern cod fishery off Atlantic Canada, or illegal tuna long lines that destroy untold numbers of turtles, seabirds and sharks. As a man of the sea, Tim sympathizes, but he does not consider himself part of the problem.

OPPOSITE: Kami, the 19-year-old daughter of Captain Tim, is now something of a veteran of the summer run. She's been helping on the boat since she was a toddler.
BELOW: Tanner and I chill out, as we wait for our turn to set the nets once more.

There's a very natural rhythm to life at sea. Intensive bouts of activity are followed by moments of calm and the chance to take a quick rest, or grab another snack. At the height of the season they don't stop so often, but as we're now coming towards the end of their hundred-day marathon, there's a playful atmosphere on board. It's flat calm; the sun is strong. There's beer in the cooler and meat, not fish, on the barbeque. The lads on board challenge me to climb, hand over hand, up the ropes. I've been duped into contests a number of times on this trip, but I'm game, and after a couple of minutes up I land back down on deck, with sore hands but happy. Tim laughs, 'I thought you'd be too old for that stuff Brucey, playing with the kids!' There's a great atmosphere on board, but I'm left feeling unsure about the nature of things. I wonder, once again, if I should give up eating such industrially caught food, however natural the process seems out here at sea.

27 AUGUST: NOME

Alaska is easily the largest state in the USA, roughly twice the size of Texas, and seven times larger than Great Britain. It has nearly 34,000 miles of tidal shoreline, longer than all the other American states combined, and harbours massive natural wealth. As well as its fisheries, there are vast reserves of timber, oil, gas and precious minerals.

OPPOSITE: We check the net for damage or snags, and then work it back into the water. Before I learned to put up my hood I got showered in jellyfish. BELOW: My home for the next part of the trip is Steve Phillip's luxury cabin on the shores of the Bering Sea. High-voltage wires are strung across the windows to keep out unwanted visitors – usually bears.

I've come to Nome, on the shores of the Bering Sea. Nome was the site of America's last gold rush in 1899, and in recent years, with the price of gold rising steeply, it's attracted a new wave of gold-diggers. I'm here to meet Steve Phillips, from Louisiana in the Deep South, who comes here for four months every year with his son Spencer searching for gold. Bouncing a few miles along the beach in what looks like a souped-up golf buggy, I arrive at their cabin, which will be my home for the next week. Steve and Spencer are part of a small eccentric community of souls who make camp here each summer, the remnants of America's last great gold rush.

When gold was discovered here at the turn of the last century, over 20,000 prospectors stampeded into these hills to stake their claims. They made their way to the shore after gold was found on the beaches. 'These guys were entrepreneurs, for certain,' Steve tells me, as we walk down to the shore. 'Just a shovel and a pan, with a spirit of adventure, and there you go, you had a business.' From the sea's edge up to the tundra, each man was given a strip of land a shovel's width either side of him, and that is where fortunes were made. 'Tents covered the beach Bruce, even in the summer the whole place looked like it was a blanket of snow.'

Today, the tents are long gone. There's an echo of history here, ghosts of the past. Nowadays, the beach gold has gone, but it can still be found on the sea bed and it's brought up using ingenious homemade dredging machines. As Steve explains, you can't buy a dredge, you have to build your own, and his design has evolved over eighteen years of trial and error. The miners dive down to the seabed and use a long hose

OPPOSITE: 'Do you want to earn some gold today, Bruce?' – Steve, the Louisiana gold hunter.
BELOW: Driftwood debris from the great Alaskan forests gathers on the isolated shoreline. The nearest trees are a hundred miles away.

to suck up the sand. It's essentially extreme vacuum cleaning on the sea floor, but far from being a chore it's rich in potential. In freezing temperatures and terrible visibility they spend all day moving rocks and sucking up the silt into their sluice box on the surface, where the tiny specks of gold collect. Gold is nineteen times heavier than water, and gets deposited into a series of sieves and mats at the bottom of the box.

But dredging at sea is a risky business, and things can easily go wrong. One of the miners has already run into trouble just after launching. His engine has failed in the middle of the breakers and he has to turn around and head back to land. Luckily there's plenty of help on hand today, but normally these men are out here on their own, and even the smallest of problems can quickly become life threatening. Not to be outdone, our man swears a little for our camera then swaps his kit onto another floating pontoon, and he's back in the water in no time at all. That pretty much sums up the energy out here – there's no time to waste, no time to 'pussy foot around', you've got to be adaptable and tough to make it. You 'get on or get out', says Steve.

In the last five years the price of gold has tripled to over $1,200/ounce, providing a very strong incentive to brave the cold waves. On a very good day they might find 5–10 ounces, so the whole scheme is not quite as mad as it might at first seem.

The number of people who come here dredging has also increased rapidly, old-timer and young'un, alike, all chasing the promise of a fortune. I feel quickly at home in Steve's cabin and I'm treated to some good old Southern hospitality. Steve is an intriguing man, highly educated, yet set in his ways. He's a great guy to talk to, always keen for big conversation and debate. He's articulate, but plays up to being 'a Southern red-neck' (his words) to lull one into thinking they're winning the point, and then he trounces us with history and statistics. It's his favourite game. He used to own an office machinery company, but sold it just before computers struck the business flat. The world changed overnight. He didn't just move with the times though, he moved away. He'd been channel-hopping late one night and had seen a cable show about gold in Alaska. He knew instantly that this is where he wanted to be, to give the outdoor life a go. That was twenty years ago. A lot of people came, struggled for a season, and had to give it all up as conditions got tough, even before the sea froze over. But Steve stuck it out and he keeps coming back.

In the distance, up and down the beach, there are isolated little cabins, most looking like a stack of old boards huddling together, as if trying to escape the bitter wind. Steve's cabin is uniquely plush. It's a pre-fabricated, corrugated metal hut of decent proportions, with raised beds in each corner on platforms above head height. The whole space is like living in a super garden shed, its walls lined with everything a Louisiana gold dredger may ever want. Steve does all the cooking and the kitchen area is well stocked. The opposite corner is the shower and heating contraption, which works very well sucking water from a bucket and over a gas-lit heating coil to warm the water. Bliss. Diving gear is strewn everywhere except on the dining table where there's a small TV screen for playing DVDs, but it's never switched on. There's just too much to be done. Our private stuff is kept by the old US Army cots we're sleeping in. Outside are the gas grill and storeroom and a surprisingly well-kept loo where all our waste is collected and burnt with oil.

On the ground nearby lie tremendous piles of 'man stuff', like flotsam washed up on the shore. Band saws, drills, engines and tyres, a couple of beat-up old snow mobiles. 'You never know when something might come in handy,' Steve says. 'It would be a pain having to wait on a spare part.' The tool shed houses oxyacetylene welding torches, angle-grinders and lathes. This is no idle DIY. All around the hut is a web of white wire lines connected to a high-voltage supply to keep away any unwanted grizzly visitors. Before this device had been erected a couple of bears had come to investigate one year and crawled through one window and out the next, trashing everything in their wake. 'Darned uncivilized to not leave through the way they came in,' he jokes.

Nome got its name when the headland was marked on an early map as '? Name', in other words, they were unsure of its name. When that map was facsimilied, the '?' was confused for the letter 'c', likewise the 'a' of 'name' read as an 'o'. '? Name' became 'C. Nome', so the story goes, and the name Cape Nome has stuck ever since. Steve laughs when he tells me this. 'Typical bureaucracy that, always getting in the way, mucking things up!'

Most gold rush areas I've been to – including, I suppose, Fort McMurray in the Canadian Tar Sands – people arrive to make money and have no intention of staying. Most seem not to particularly enjoy the work. Here, however, most of these guys actually seem to love the finding of the gold as much, if not more, than actually having it. After making his fortune from his office business, Steve expanded into diving stores. He's now 'semi-retired' – again his words. He could be taking it easy down South, but he's up here because he wants to be. Simple as that. Steve pulls a book down from a shelf. In it he finds some lines by Robert Service, a couple of verses from the famous poem 'Spell of the Yukon'. It seemed to sum it all up perfectly:

I wanted the gold, and I sought it,
I scrabbled and mucked like a slave.
Was it famine or scurvy – I fought it;
I hurled my youth into a grave.

THIS PAGE: We help Spencer bring his gold-dredging raft back onto the shore.

I wanted the gold and I got it –
Came out with a fortune last fall,
Yet somehow life's not what I thought it,
And somehow the gold isn't all.

There's gold, and it's haunting and haunting;
It's luring me on as of old;
Yet it isn't the gold that I'm wanting
So much as just finding the gold.
It's the great, big, broad land 'way up yonder,
It's the forests where silence has lease;
It's the beauty that thrills me with wonder,
It's the stillness that fills me with peace.

THESE PAGES: And now it's my turn. These ingenious contraptions are part pontoon raft, part suction machine. It's a floating hoover, and does the job brilliantly.

28 AUGUST: NOME

The next morning the sea looks pretty rough, and I'm slightly nervous about the prospect of going diving. I'm hoping for a chance to test the water, but it's not looking promising. While we're chatting, Steve warns me about the strict rules of etiquette that apply to gold dredging. Some of the more experienced miners have already braved the conditions this morning and are now heading back to shore. With Steve's advice ringing in my ears I'm careful not to ask how much gold they've found and wait to be invited to look in the sluice box to check out their latest haul. To ask to see before being beckoned over, he tells me, 'would be like asking to see his wife getting undressed. You might see what you want but he's not gonna be real happy with you!'

The clouds soon roll in, the weather turns foul, and we've missed our chance to go out today. I'm not too bothered as I wasn't so mad about a polar swim just yet and Steve's snug cabin is really appealing after some long weeks of travelling. We hunker down to talk, read books and drink tea. The crew take advantage of the break in play to run through some of the footage we've already shot on this trip. There's time to snooze, make a call home, to have a shave. Small, but wonderful, these things are luxuries in our usually crazy schedule.

The next day, however, it looks like we're game on. Ever the gold-dredger's sergeant major, Steve wakes me up with barked orders and a mug of coffee you could stand a spoon in. As I struggle to open my eyes, I find his face inches from mine. He's laughing and shouting at the same time: 'Do you want to earn some gold today, Bruce, do you want to really earn it? No pussying around with the camera crew, holding everything up. If so get up now, I'm going to work you till your fingers bleed!' I know he's playing up for my benefit, but also I know he doesn't want me to let him down. I have to step up.

I have to confess I'm a little nervous as I suit up: this is quite unlike any diving I've done before. We're sitting a couple of hundred metres off shore on this Heath-Robinson floating raft, all pipes and fastenings, rusty nails and rubber tubing. For a lone pilot who knows the risk, who is competent and happy to take them, it's a perfect machine. To me it looks like it's held together with string. For this though, I loved these guys. A health-and-safety executive would be driven to madness seeing one of these contraptions, and I know Steve and the boys here would have a few choice words for such an overprotective official if one ever strayed this far north.

The oxygen is pumped down a tube from the dredge on the surface and hot water is fed through another tube into my wetsuit to keep me from hypothermia. Steve goes down first to do a quick recce of the seabed and check if there's any gold to be seen. Normally the divers go down alone. As I'm a novice, Spencer, who is a fully trained instructor, has agreed to be my buddy. Down at the bottom the visibility is no more than a couple of feet and it takes me a little while to get my bearings. It's seriously cold and the currents are strong, but I just have to concentrate on sticking the hose in the sand and sucking it all up, being careful not to hoover up any starfish along the way. We are not that deep – maybe only 5 metres – but with all the sand being disturbed, the light of my torch sends beams through the murky water. I'm spending most of my time trying not to get caught in the pipes or trip up over the rocks. I can't really tell what's going up into the sluice box, but I hope there's a few flecks of gold in there to show for my efforts.

It's hard physical work, and after I've been down for almost an hour, Steve decides to call it a day. We clamber up into the boat, remove our masks, and turn off the pumps. Bent over the sluice box, as the swell rocks the pontoon boat, we can all make out the tiny flecks of gold. Not glistening, but bright against the flat greys of the mud and silt. I can see Steve is pleased. He pours the contents of the sluice into a plastic bucket for me to take ashore. 'That's your bean money Bruce. A good honest day's work for you.'

Back in the hut, Steve is teasing me as we pan and clean the remainder of the mud I've collected from the sea floor. He's not expecting much, but after half an hour's more filtering and washing we have a small handful of treasured flakes. We measure it carefully. It's about four penny weight, about $200 worth. Though I've enjoyed the experience, it's not the gold that matters. More precious to me is having the chance to be in the company of people who are passionate about what they do. I love Steve for coming up here for months at a time, following a dream, a promise. Embracing the land, with eyes open to the adventure and the toughness of the life. Steve doesn't need to be here financially, he is already a wealthy man. But, he comes year on year, because it is something he enjoys doing. He's able to find something in this wilderness that he can't find at home. It's freedom, the beauty of rugged nature; it's fresh air and hope. He spends time with his son. All that means so much more than gold.

5 SEPTEMBER: PRUDHOE BAY

I'm flying north across the Arctic Circle towards the oil fields that have made Alaska one of the richest states in America. Though generally considered to be a wilderness, it's a state with revenues so large it competes with many of the world's major nations. Cruising over the stately Brooks Range, and coming in across the vast sweep of tundra, far to the north I finally get a glimpse of Prudhoe Bay and out to the Beaufort Sea. The North Slope deposits here, that have in the last decade driven almost 90 per cent of the economy, are slowly but surely drying up. The industry is now looking beyond the land, turning their attention out into the Arctic Ocean. Like the gold, the new frontier is the seabed. Recent exploration has revealed massive new reserves off-shore. But the local people are concerned that any oil spills under the sea ice would have a devastating impact on the wildlife and especially the bowhead whales on which they depend.

2010 is on track to be the warmest year in the Arctic on record, and this summer the sea ice is melting at a near-record pace. The more the sun heats this newly open water the longer it will take to refreeze in the winter. As a result, the thinner ice will

THIS PAGE: Up and down the coast, dredgers for all shapes and sizes continue their hunt for gold.

OVERLEAF: A truck drives along an ice road which links Nuiqsut Alpine Oilfield to Prudhoe Bay. The difficulties of providing infrastructure to support Arctic offshore rigs could have catastrophic consequences in an emergency.
FOLLOWING PAGES: We turn in for the night as the sun sinks low beneath the horizon in Kaktovik.

melt more easily next summer. This is the spiral of decline for the Arctic sea ice. Scientists are still uncertain exactly what the timescale is, over which a major part of the Arctic Ocean changes from sunlight-reflecting ice to dark, sunlight-absorbing open water, but many are sure that it will spell problems for us all. There is still the hope that the trend will reverse and the sea ice will recover, but the ocean-atmosphere system is so complicated it is impossible to know exactly how, why or when. But the long-term trend does seem to be for warming, which means melting year on year. Though this should make us fearful, not least for the environment, this melting is opening up possibilities for the oil industry.

At the same time, warm Pacific Ocean water is pulsing through the Bering Strait into the Arctic basin, helping to melt the sea ice between the Alaskan coast and eastern Siberia. Scientists are just beginning to understand how this newly exposed open water will change the movement of heat energy and major air currents across the Arctic, in turn producing winds that in time may push the remaining sea ice across into the Atlantic. New patterns of wind could also disturb the jet streams into Europe, which are apparently weakening and moving northward. This could increase storm intensity, disrupt rainfall patterns and thus alter food production far to the south. Changes to the ice here may cause crop failure in Europe or even East Asia.

It is impossible to get a handle on all of this – even the greatest experts have a major job on their hands, and my head starts to swim when I begin reading through all the data that is now available. We can be sure that changes here will affect all of us. It's hard sometimes to imagine this, staring out over empty tundra or across an icy fjord as I have done these last few months. The Arctic is not remote and irrelevant, but is really taking on a vital significance.

Yet, even more worrying still in my view, is that our governments have reached something of a standstill on climate policy. All around the world there seem to be indications that our climate is changing, and I have seen evidence of this on my travels and through conversations with the people I have met. Weather events are becoming increasingly unpredictable: I think of the terrible floods and devastating mudslides in China, freak snowstorms in America this winter, or heatwaves in Russia. Something must be the cause of all this? Yet in my opinion the political consensus seems to have fallen away and the issues have become pulled in different directions by different voices and interests. In Canada, Japan, Australia and countries in Europe, the global economic crisis and other domestic problems have taken priority over climate issues. For China and India, economic growth and energy security are more pressing concerns. Here in the USA, the Senate has decided for now not to push for approval of a climate bill.

It's just a few months ago, on 30 May, that the USA declared a six-month moratorium on all deepwater offshore drilling activities on its 'outer continental shelf'.

This enforced suspension was in direct response to the horrendous Deepwater Horizon spill, which has blighted the waters of the Gulf of Mexico with an estimated 53,000 barrels of crude oil per day escaping into the marine environment. As I write this, up here in Alaska, they still haven't managed to stop the flow or contain the resulting oil slick. The long-term impact on the ecology and the fisheries in the region is impossible to estimate, but right now it's fairly straightforward for the people on the ground and at sea to appreciate. The largest marine oil spill in the history of the petroleum industry, it will likely continue to have a devastating effect on the ecosystem there for many years to come. The Cabana family in Prince William Sound say that the ecosystem is still suffering from the Exxon Valdez spill there twenty years ago. The herring, for example, has never returned.

I hope that this disaster may have a positive result – that it may be the proof that we need to proceed with caution in our exploration of these deepwater sites. The world's remaining oil reserves are in areas where extraction will be difficult and increasingly risky. I hope that our experience of the Gulf disaster will encourage other nations to consider putting prospective drilling operations on hold and subjecting them and existing sites to more rigorous regulations, while increasing their committment to developing alternative energy sources to the burning of fossil fuels. I personally don't think we can afford to take the environmental risk of drilling in the remote Arctic, an area known for some of the most hostile weather conditions on the planet. Though the sea ice may be melting, 20-foot seas and gale-force winds can batter the region for days on end. The difficulties multiply exponentially in deep water, not to mention when conditions are so challenging topside.

Even if nothing were to go wrong, there will be unavoidable impacts in each phase of development in the Arctic Ocean – drilling, seismic explorations, production platforms, pipelines, terminals and tankers – all contributing to significant disturbances in the coastal and marine ecosystems. The Exxon Valdez oil spill in Alaska caused the death of over 250,000 seabirds the year it happened and even today some two-thirds of the fish and wildlife populations injured by the oil spill have yet to fully recover – twenty-one years later. History proves that humans do make mistakes, and equipment does sometimes fail.

Risks will be taken that we do not yet understand. Drifting ice, inhuman temperatures and winter darkness make much of the region inaccessible. If a blowout like the Gulf BP disaster did happen in the Arctic, mobilizing a response would be virtually impossible. There is no infrastructure to support a serious cleanup operation if one were needed, no big ports or large airfields. The closest Coast Guard station might be over 1,000 kilometres away. When you consider that the Gulf emergency operation has been postponed frequently because of poor conditions and high seas, it could be months before a spill could be brought under control. Oil would travel with

OFFSHORE OIL The current trend of melting of the sea ice in the Arctic Ocean suggests that one day it will become extensive enough to allow for previously impossible energy and resource exploration and development. Though predictions of summer ice completely disappearing within a few years are now regarded as pessimistic, it is highly likely that within a generation offshore extraction will become practicable and economically viable here. The Arctic seabed is said to contain one quarter of the world's mineral riches. The temptations are huge, the stakes high.

A country has the right to exploit oil and minerals in an 'Exclusive Economic Zone' up to 200 nautical miles (370 kilometres) from the edge of its continental shelf. It can also make a claim if it can be proven that their submerged territory extends beyond 200 miles. There are a number of different ways of 'carving' up the Arctic Ocean region – a

Although Russia is no doubt leading the way, America and Canada are also acting fast. In the summer of 2010 they each sent Coast Guard ships on a joint data-finding mission to the energy-rich Beaufort Sea, to help determine the extent of their continental shelves. Canada, in particular, feels that it must assert its sovereignty over what it regards as its share of the Arctic. It has increased its military presence there, investing in a new fleet of ice-strengthened patrol boats and tabling plans for a network of deep-water harbours. Ships now have to apply to Canada for permits if they want to navigate the Northwest Passage, the maze of ice-choked islands which make up the northern coastline and which Canada regards as an internal waterway. The UN, however, says it is an international sea and as such should be free for traffic, however difficult this is currently.

straight line to a central point such as the North Pole can be drawn and the disupted area sliced up, a bit like cutting a cake. A median or equidistant line could also be drawn around the nearest point of a country's coastline.

In the future, all claims over the Arctic will have to be made to the United Nations under the terms of the Convention on the Law of the Sea, with disputes settled in an orderly way within a clear international legal framework. So, it's not a race as such, but nations are nonetheless vying with each other to gather evidence to establish the full nature of their territorial rights and to develop the equipment to make offshore extraction here a reality. The possibility of a seasonally ice-free sea in the Arctic is the largest environmental state-change on Earth and it brings potential economic, cultural and political instabilities as well as opportunities that could have global implications.

In the future, as the sea ice retreats, possibilities increase. Canadian Prime Minister Stephen Harper went on a tour of the Arctic this summer, declaring: 'We live in a time of renewed foreign interest in Canada's Arctic. With foreign aircraft probing the skies, vessels plying northern waters, and the eyes of the world gazing our way, we must remain vigilant.'

According to recent figures, the seabed below a disputed area of the Beaufort Sea, for example, is eye-wateringly rich in resources, containing a potential 1.7 billion cubic metres of natural gas – enough to supply the whole of Canada for twenty years – and an additional 1 billion cubic metres of oil. Both the USA and Canada will likely emerge from any future negotiation with the benefit of substantial holdings.

currents in and under sea ice and it would be impossible to contain. The lack of bacteria at colder temperatures also means that the oil residues would not break down as in warmer southern seas. The consequences here could be catastrophic, not only for the species in this fragile and vital ecosystem – the whales, the walruses, the bears, birds and fish – but also for the Alaskan native people who depend on the sea for their way of life.

7 September: Kaktovik

The village of Kaktovik sits perched on the very edge of the North American continent, on the shores of the Beaufort Sea. It falls within the Arctic National Wildlife Refuge and is home to the Inupiat, also known as the 'whale people'. This tiny inaccessible village of just 250 inhabitants is strategically established on the annual migration route of the bowhead whale, which has fed the Inupiat here for almost 5,000 years.

My first impressions are that it's a fairly bleak, isolated place, and its residents are not overly forthcoming. The people here are very conscious of the outside world's opposition to their whaling customs. They're fed up with foreigners flying in and passing judgement and they're fearful that public opinion could force them to stop. They have everything to lose and little to gain from publicity, at least that's what they think. No surprise, they're quite suspicious of incomers, especially film crews. I spend most of my first evening in town hopeful but frustrated in the guest house where we are staying. I'm not living with a family this time, but, besides the crew, just have my laptop for company. I try to catch up on my journal and read over some of my notes about the next week's shooting. It's clear, though, that any plans are useless without local support for what we are trying to do. It is hard to travel where other people have gone, to visit communities whose feelings have already been hardened by the opinions of misinformed southerners. I turn in for the night, hoping for a positive start in the morning.

Conditions out at sea are not good for hunting today, so I get a chance to try to make friends before the whaling begins. There is one family that has kindly agreed to meet me. Eddie works as a tour guide for the limited tourist trade that comes here, and as such is more open to meeting outsiders. Eddie explains that filming the whale hunt itself is not allowed in Inupiat culture. 'It's maybe not so much culture now though, it's really just that we've been hurt in the past,' Eddie tells me, as his wife Marie comes out to join us. 'It's just that we don't always know where a film team comes from, or what they're gonna use the film for. They often have different agendas and sometimes they make the community misrepresented. That's why you will encounter reluctance, maybe even anger, when you go around town with a camera.'

The Inupiat believe that the whale will only give itself to them if they are properly prepared. Out of respect for the whale, Eddie has to clean out his traditional ice cellar to ensure the success of the hunt. I join him and lend a hand shifting frozen chunks of meat around in the darkness. His father carved this space in the permafrost, and it is constantly below freezing. But as Eddie explains, 'some folks can't use theirs now. The permafrost is melting. The meat is ruined.' I stack a couple of caribou legs into a pile, next to a bucket containing the head. We use a shovel and crowbar to dislodge a ringed seal and move it towards the back. 'The cellar has to be clear, so we can store our meat as soon as it's caught, so it's part a necessity to survive, but also part to show our respect for the animal. If a man is lazy he doesn't deserve to kill a whale. But, you know, we don't get to choose who captures the whale – the whale decides.'

Due to family reasons, Eddie and Marie will not be whaling this year, and rather worryingly I've yet to meet anyone that is. Three of the five whaling captains have said they want nothing to do with us, and the other two have said they're too busy to be filmed. It's always a little arrogant to come into a community and expect people to make room for strangers in their lives. This is a constant issue with filming, and so it's important to gain permissions upfront. I take a walk along the beach as fog begins to roll in from the north. There's a damp chill to the air now, summer is giving way to autumn. This rubbish weather doesn't help my spirits. It's strange, I'm here trying to learn more about a people, and the camera crew does me no favours at all. I feel a sense of isolation that I've rarely felt before within a tribe. I try to retreat into my thoughts but feel dishevelled, unbalanced in some way. I try to be patient, to sit it out.

THIS PAGE: The beach, a mile or so beyond Kaktovik, is littered with a pile of whale bones, like a sombre graveyard to these majestic creatures.

THIS PAGE: My first encounter with a polar bear in the wild. The cub comes to within a few feet of us, before my guide encourages him away. It's a magical experience for me, one I'll always treasure.

I can't even call friends from home as only a few understand what I'm trying to do. Mere mention of the word whaling seems to generate all sorts of emotional responses and prejudgements. And so here I am with the crew, and we're not getting much done and we are all frustrated. I think it may prove impossible for us to be accepted here. We have decided to put our cameras down and try to make friends.

9 September: Kaktovik

The people of Kaktovik aren't the only ones waiting anxiously for the whale hunt to begin. Next morning, determined to cheer up, I'm with Eddie and his friend Bruce on our way to the beaches that surround the village where every year the whalebones are left out for the Inupiat's hungry neighbours. The polar bears swim all the way here from the Arctic pack ice, up to 200 miles to the north, perhaps more. At this time of year there are very few seals around, so the exhausted bears gather in large numbers, waiting for the whale scraps to appear.

We follow some paw prints in the shingle, past another wide inlet. Eddie instantly reaches for his gun, not to hunt but for our protection, as just a couple of hundred metres away there are three bears lying close to the ground. They spotted us long before we were aware of their presence. They make no sound, just raise their

snouts in the air, catching our smell on the breeze. One of the youngsters has seen us and is curious. In seconds, he begins to trot over for a closer look. I don't know whether to stand still, or to run away. As it is, I stay completely still, unable to move, not scared, but entranced. Everything happens now in slow motion. The young bear comes to within 5 feet of our group, before Eddie makes a gentle noise and he turns almost immediately on his heels. His mother gestures with her head and they all pad off in the opposite direction. It's my first experience of polar bears in the wild and to have them approach so close is an unbelievable privilege. We slowly retreat back up the beach, making no undue sounds, but eyeing them as we leave.

Our unforgettable experience with the young polar bears seems to have brought us some luck. Marie has arranged for me to have dinner with her cousin, James Lampe, who is one of the five whaling captains in the village. The doors in the community are slowly starting to open. I'm with James, his wife Glenda, Marie and her daughter Flora, who have come together for a family meal before he leaves for the hunt. After dinner, as the family relax, the conversation turns to whaling. Even though we now have permission to film, some people are clearly unhappy about us being here.

James is busy preparing the harpoons for the day. He's been a whaling captain for just a few years now, after his father – a renowned captain – passed him the responsi-

bility, but James has yet to catch his first whale. It would mean a huge amount to him and to his family. This is not sport, but a rite of passage and a way of connecting to his ancestors. He describes how they once hunted by hand in seal-skin boats. Individual hunters in their single kayaks would gather in teams to locate and surround a whale, reaching from their paddles to throw their ivory-ended harpoons in a rapid and dynamic attack. Sometimes they would take to larger boats – the *umiak* – with men and women paddling to help tow the whale back to shore, often many miles away. It was a hugely dangerous and exhausting undertaking. Many people did not return alive. James is rightly proud of the skills of the past. But the whale hunt is also a key part of his family's nourishment in the present. Without the meat from the whale, all of the families here would find it very difficult to afford to keep living here – the place where they were born and where their people have always lived.

Though skin boats have long since been replaced by metal speedboats with outboard motors, the risks are still severe. James shows me some of his father's old equipment. Nowadays the whale is actually killed by an explosive head that blows up inside it. Even this harpoon technology is quite old now and they're stuck with a choice whether to upgrade or not. If they upgrade, they would be losing some of their credence as old-style hunters, a part of the argument to allow them to maintain their tradition. If they don't upgrade they continue to be less efficient at killing. This story is increasingly more complex the more you probe. And just how traditional is an explosive harpoon anyway? Apparently, a good hunter only needs one shot to kill a whale and it does not take too long to die. What was too long, I wondered? Twenty minutes perhaps? James wouldn't say. And what about arguments around the intelligence of whales, should we really be doing any of this? If the harpoon gun isn't cleaned properly it can be lethal to the crew, not just the unwitting whale. Five years ago James's father blew his hand off while firing the gun.

There's a strange quietness in the air just before whaling. As they wish each other good luck for the hunt, everyone is aware of the many dangers to be faced out at sea. It's an intimate moment. As the sun is just appearing, James's crew jump in the boat, wave a last goodbye and then push away from shore. All five boats have now left. Families gather to listen at their radios. Glenda is a nurse at the local clinic and she brings me to her workplace, but her thoughts are obviously elsewhere. Hearts and minds are not in town, but with loved ones out at sea. There are certain strict taboos surrounding the hunt, so when you're listening to the radio you have to keep quiet out of respect for the whale. The whole village waits in anticipation.

A few hours later the hunters return empty-handed, solemn and disappointed. After hours of searching there were no whales to be seen. The sea was rough and they couldn't even keep track of each other, let alone spot the whale. The next morning the whalers head out to sea again to try their luck. We arrive too late to see

OPPOSITE: These young polar bears have come a long way from their winter dens, by sea and shore, to reach the village and wait for the whale feast.

THIS PAGE: We gather on the beach at dawn as the last boat sets off in search of a whale. Five boats went out, but I'm confined to shore.

them go. Still few people are talking to us, but we just make out the last boat clearing the bay and heading out into the fog. We wait, like everyone else. Glenda's radio is on, but for hours there is no sound. I begin to doze off, but am awakened by a faint crackle and then a murmured voice, quiet but clear. 'Right now in this place, boats gather around a whale. So we therefore give thanks.' The prayer has been sent. They have a whale.

Though it will be hours before the whale arrives, a crowd gathers on the beach, dogs race beneath our feet, young girls dance and clap their hands, whistles and cheers. There is much work to do in preparation. Many people are in tears, so happy, proud and thankful. What I'm witnessing is a modern expression of an ancient tradition. Today they use mechanical diggers to haul in the whale, but I can only imagine the human effort it took in the past. I am quite shocked by the sight of this giant creature lying low like a small island in the water, waiting to be butchered. I feel confused by the excitement it has created, but this age-old tradition is in the Inupiat blood. The whole community is celebrating not just the capture of the whale but also the safe return of the hunters.

Seeing their reactions now, you can begin to appreciate how happy people must have been in the past, what this must have meant to the community when times were tough, and the winters were very cold and very long. This represented life. I experience my strange sense of guilt at watching this, but my sadness is soon overcome by the pleasure of seeing the energy and joy that this has brought. This is a festival of what it means to have life. As soon as the whale is beached, all the children in the village climb up on top to have photographs taken by their proud parents. It seems a modern sort of pose, but it's not pride in the negative sense. It's heritage, but it's also real life. It's like a beating drum of a proud people, of a moment of real pleasure, a moment of closeness to the past.

When it's time to start butchering the whale, the crew are told to back off as the
captain doesn't want the bloody images to be seen. Respectfully, they stop immediately
and withdraw back up the beach to where the women are starting a whale-meat production line. They let me join in for an hour or so, before I rejoin Rob for some filming.
In 1977, the Inupiat were banned from hunting by the International Whaling Com-
mission. Once scientists were able to prove that the bowhead was existing in plentiful
numbers and not unduly at risk, they were eventually given an annual quota of about
seventy-five struck whales a year, a total to be shared among eleven Alaskan native villages. The whale provides much more than just food though. The whole nature of the
hunt brings the community together, it binds the Inupiat cultural identity. Today it
seems the culture is undergoing a revival of sorts, after a long period of being repressed.
The butchering continues long into the evening.

One of the last parts to be removed is the tail, which is traditionally the preserve
of the successful captain. The lucky recipient is George Kaleak and as it is dragged
away, he explains just how happy he is today, the best day of his year. He doesn't mind
my asking him questions in front of the camera. A gentle man, he feels the strength of
his traditions and won't let himself be frustrated that outsiders can't understand his
people's ways. 'People will always have different opinions, I can't stop that, but for us

this whale is a blessing. It's what we look forward to each and every year and it's what we teach our children. It's a chance for us to celebrate our food and be thankful. When was the last time you did that?'

11 September: Kaktovik

I'm with James and Glenda on the way to George's house for the whale captain's lunch. The whole community is gathering for a celebration feast. Not far away, on a hill at the edge of the village, birds fill the sky with noise and circle overhead. Trucks load up, quad bikes race back and forth. The rest of the meat is being shared out equally between the other whaling captains. Later in the afternoon, back at the Lampes' house, James's share is being delivered. It arrives by JCB and is tumbled out onto a vast tarpaulin. As a whaling captain, James is responsible for nourishing his crew, his extended family and his neighbours. Eager to help, I'm passed a meat hook, and we spend a number of hours dividing up all the meat equally among the whaling crew. Throughout the village there are piles of whale meat, each being carefully allocated. And everyone is busy chopping.

At another house, Marie and Flora are cutting the blubber off the meat and putting it aside for the polar bears. Flora's brother Eddie Junior is also lending a hand

BELOW: We were only permitted limited filming of the whale ashore. This photograph of a massive 48-foot bowhead whale was taken during a previous hunt off the Alaskan village of Barrow.
OVERLEAF: A bowhead whale swims though an open lead in the pack ice in the Chukchi Sea, off the coast of Alaska.

THE BOWHEAD WHALE

There are three major families of baleen whales. The *Mysticeti* or 'moustached whales' that cruise the cool polar waters feeding on plankton. The *Balaenopteridae* whales include the humpback, fin, minke and the largest animal ever known, the blue whale. It can grow over 30 metres long. Though it's found in all oceans, with small, recovering populations observed in the Bering Sea and Baffin Bay, the blue is still endangered. The grey whale, the only *Eschrichtiidae*, used to be seen in the Atlantic, with the animals feeding off Greenland and migrating as far south as the Bay of Biscay, but this population became extinct in the eighteenth century after over-hunting by Basque whalers. The grey whale now survives in small numbers in the North Pacific, the Chukchi and Beaufort seas.

The third family, which includes the bowhead, is the *Balaenidae*, known as 'right' whales – so called by the early whalers because they were the right whales to kill. They were large, slow swimmers, and could be easily overhauled by a rowing boat. They did not fight when harpooned and because of their huge mass of oil-yielding blubber they floated when dead, making them easier to transport to ships or to shore. As a result, these whales were hunted almost to extinction. In recent decades, with concerted global protection and the prevention of commercial whaling, populations appear to be recovering.

In waters off Alaska it is estimated there are some 12,000 bowhead whales (*balaena mysticetus*) and they are still hunted in small numbers for subsistence by native peoples. The bowhead is social and nonaggressive and it retreats under the ice when threatened. They can grow to about 18 metres in length, weighing over 100 tons. Some bowheads taken by native hunters in recent years have been found to have ancient stone harpoons embedded in them, some dated to well over 100 years old. Scientists have since investigated the animals with greater accuracy and it is suggested that some may have ages in excess of 200 hundred years, meaning that the whales rival the giant tortoise as the longest living animals on this planet.

But, rapid changes to our oceans put the longevity of whales under real threat. The warming trend and decreased salinity levels will cause a significant shift in the location and abundance of plankton and krill, the whale's main food sources. Migration patterns, based on ocean temperature and circulation, will also be disrupted by a warming Arctic. The ever-increasing amount of ocean noise, including sonar, drowns out vocalization produced by many of the whale families, which makes it harder for them to communicate. Research has clearly shown that bowhead whales off Alaska are being disturbed from preferred habitat areas when there is noise from seismic exploration by oil companies.

and they're discussing how much the bowhead whale means to the community. 'It's by far the most important thing we do every year', young Eddie tells me. 'It's really the happiest time for everyone, the only time we really all get together. Some people say we should be looking to get money from oil instead. They say we should surrender our hunting to make dollars on a rig. We are not damaging the whale populations here, or the environment. But if there's an oil spill, if it's in the winter, how can they clean it up?'

On my last night in the village we head out to the bone pile on the beach, where there's a small crowd of villagers watching the bears enjoying their long-awaited feast. The Inupiat have a relationship of real respect with their four-legged Arctic neighbours and despite the inherent dangers of having them so close to the village, they're happy to share their harvest with them. Most of the bears arrive here exhausted, malnourished after months of swimming and searching for food. The Inupiat give them something back. By daybreak the bears are gone; life continues here for one more year.

It's also time for me to leave and continue my Arctic journey. Like the fishermen I met in the south, and the gold miners in Nome, the Inupiat people are harvesting the riches of the sea. But, unlike the others I have met, they don't catch more than they need and they don't make a profit. They don't sell nature; they celebrate it. It's not gold, but it's immeasurably more valuable, I think. It's been such an important few days for the community in Kaktovik. I came here carrying my preconceptions and full of opinions of a people that were based on misunderstandings. I couldn't have been more wrong. The Inupiat whalers are a gentle, open-hearted people who are still close to the natural world in a very real and meaningful way. There is so much warmth here. To catch a whale is a vital part of their heritage and culture. To have respect for what you eat, that's something we should all try to understand. We shouldn't be too quick to judge. They have a spiritual relationship with this animal that has sustained them for thousands of years through the long Arctic winter. I, for one, hope the outside world can see this connection.

The potential impacts from offshore drilling in Alaska's waters should concern all of us. Any resultant pollution will lock fishermen out of their livelihoods. People are fighting to get food on their tables even now, and we must not imagine a future where they are unable to eat from the waters they have fished for generations. The indigenous people in this area are not anti-development, it's just that they have to live with the consequences of industrial growth. Alaskan waters provide billions of dollars in seafood every year. The Inupiat of the North Slope go whale hunting each season to feed their communities and to maintain their culture. These resources are renewable, if properly managed and respected. Oil drilling is not. I think it is too much of a gamble to take.

OPPOSITE ABOVE: Traditions are upheld here despite modern influences. The whale's tail, taken away by a digger, is the prize for the successful captain.
OPPOSITE BELOW: As soon as the whale is hauled ashore, amid huge celebrations, children climb on its back to have their photographs taken.

NORWAY

THIS PAGE: A Sámi *lavvu* – the traditional tent in modern materials – one of several homes for me during this final leg of my Arctic journey.

Norway
THE NORTHERN LIGHTS

'Ny-Ålesund is both a fantastic place and a great idea — to collect many different disciplines and many different nationalities in one single place to research together. Culturally and scientifically this is the challenge to point us in directions where we can do good things together to increase knowledge for mankind.'

Winter is approaching. The last leg of my travels takes me closer to home, to the European Arctic. I say closer to home, I'm still going to be travelling out into challenging environments, but these are my final journeys before a welcome rest. Our film begins in the northern city of Tromsø, a bustling urban centre on the edge of the Arctic Ocean. Beyond the bright lights of this fascinating place, I will be heading out to live with the Sámi people. I meet today's reindeer herders, equipped with motorbikes and helicopters, and I want to experience a little of how their cultural ways are changing as each year passes. I'm also going to head further north to Svalbard to spend some time with one of the Arctic's new tribes: the international scientists who make their home there in isolated research stations. I want to learn more about the hard science and the truths of climate change from the experts. I also want to get a sense of what it's like to live further north than anyone else on Earth.

Though Arctic Norway is the main focus of our film, I'm also longing to return to Russia, this huge and mystifying nation, once again. After filming in Siberia this summer, and having travelled in the middle of winter with the Nenet reindeer people when I was making my *Tribe* series, we all agree that we really should go back. Over

half the Arctic coastline is in Russia and it has become the major player on the polar geopolitical scene, so we felt it was right we make a section of our last film here. We'll be travelling from Arkhangelsk by train and off-road truck to reach the small village of Nyukhcha to live with the Komi people. Our camera crew is hoping for lots of folk tales, wood craft, mushroom collecting and vodka swilling. We shall see. The grist in the mill, however, is that the forest here is dying – and no one really knows why. We've been in touch with a few experts in Finland and Russia who say they suspect climate change but admit that no one understands the full complexity of this ecosystem.

21 September: Longyearbyen

Two days in the UK after our Alaska shoot, dropping off film and checking in with our team, was all I had to rest before heading northward once again. I'm now in the beautiful archipelago of Svalbard in the High Arctic, a place I've wanted to visit for some time. We are a few hundred miles beyond mainland Europe, midway between Norway and the North Pole and level with the north coast of Greenland. It's the

highest latitude I've ever been to, a fraction above Qaanaaq where our Arctic journey began.

Though easily reached now by plane or ship, this island group still feels remote. Early humans never made it here. In more recent history it's been variously occupied and settled by whalers, miners and the military and, most recently, a growing cohort of international scientists. Svalbard's past and present offers us lessons for land claims and cooperation in the Far North.

This place has been disputed, especially between the Norwegians and Russians, for many decades and the British, Germans, Swedish, Canadians and others have all been here over the years. Dutch ships first came in 1596, intent on expanding their trading empire and discovering a Northeast Passage to the riches of China. They named the islands 'Spitsbergen', the steep mountains, and although the expedition ended in disaster, it turned the attentions of the world to this remote place. The warm current here that keeps the west coast of Svalbard ice-free and nutrient rich is an ideal habitat for capelin, shrimp, cod and herring, and so too walrus, seals and whales. Nav-

ABOVE: The remote settlement of Ny-Ålesund has become home to a new Arctic tribe – international scientists.

ABOVE: A memorial to Roald Amundsen greets us, a connection to Norway's past, but this settlement is also looking to the future.

igating the waters here in 1612, one British captain reported that there were so many whales in the sound that they were impossible to count. Before long, other nations came here to exploit the seas. In the beginning the hunts were seasonal, with most taking place in the fjords or close to shore around small whaling stations where the meat was butchered and the oil boiled in large copper pots. In time, these stations grew in size and men stayed all year. Large ships replaced small boats. Explosive harpoons improved on those thrown by hand. Techniques became sophisticated and more successful. But by the beginning of the eighteenth century it was all over. The Greenland right whales had been hunted to the verge of extinction.

The Russians also moved in, focusing their efforts on the walrus, polar bear and fox. And after them came the prospectors, making their fortunes from the outcrops of coal. In 1920 a treaty gave Norway governance over the islands, which until that time had been a 'no man's land', obliging them to preserve the natural environment and prohibiting military development. During the Second World War the Germans invaded Norway and evacuated the entire archipelago. The mines fell silent for a while, although they are running again today. Tourism is another mainstay of the economy and the government of Norway spends hundreds of millions of kroner each year to maintain the scientific infrastructure here and to uphold the integrity of its leadership in the region. Today more than half of the archipelago is protected by a national park and various other plant and animal reserves and refuges. There are lessons here for all of us.

We flew from Tromsø to Longyearbyen and joined a boat bound for Ny-Ålesund, where we arrived in the early hours of the following morning. At daybreak we see a beautiful fjord with snow-capped peaks all around and the sea as still as can be; mirror-like, the absence of a single ripple, almost implausibly serene. The sun was low and, as it was close to equinox, we had equal hours of day and night. Amazingly, within a month, it'll be 24 hours of night as the polar winter envelops everything. We'll be losing about a quarter of an hour of daylight each day.

The first face I see is a familiar one. I'm greeted by a bust of legendary Norwegian explorer Roald Amundsen, proudly positioned in front of the base. The man who so famously beat Captain Scott in the race to the South Pole was also the first to navigate the Northwest Passage. In 1926, he joined the Italian engineer Umberto Nobile over fly to the North Pole in an airship, leaving Ny-Ålesund bound for those barren, gold-rich beaches of Alaska where I had been just last month. Their 'Rome to Nome' flight was a milestone in aviation history, a triumph of technological ingenuity and daring to think the impossible. But the story would end in tragedy, two years later. Nobile and his crew went missing on a second flight and Amundsen set off in a plane to find them. He was never seen again.

The world's most northerly permanent settlement, about forty full-time residents live here in Ny-Ålesund on the west coast of Spitsbergen, the largest island in the Svalbard group. It's a former coal-mining village, turned international research station, a 'natural laboratory'. Most of the inhabitants are foreigners. The German, French and Chinese scientists are here pretty much year-round alongside their Norwegian hosts. The day I arrive a few of the Italians and the Japanese are gathering their gear together to leave as winter draws in. There had been Dutch, Koreans and some Brits here too, to swell the numbers of this intriguing tribe to about 200 during the short summer. Add to that the cruise ships and film crews that wash up from time to time and you have a sense of the place.

Up on Zeppelin Mountain, 474 metres above sea level, the Swedes are collaborating with the Norwegians in a remarkable atmospheric research station. At this height the sensors experience minimal interference from the main base below and the data, measured continuously by the scientists here, is being used all over the world. We reach the station via a quaint cable car, and the views at the top are fantastic. The weather is kind to us today. Inside, there's an intriguing array of computer monitors and sensing equipment, all humming away in unison, quietly detecting about 160 chemicals and contaminants. The Zeppelin station has instruments sensitive enough to detect cigarette smoke 2 kilometres away, I'm told. Scientists here, led by Professor Kim Holmén, Research Director of the Norwegian Polar Institute in Tromsø, have been monitoring the increase of several greenhouse gases in the atmosphere. Using as a baseline the amount of carbon dioxide (CO_2) in 1860 (the earliest reliable date, scientists say) as 290 parts per million (ppm), they have found that it has reached an annual average of 375 ppm, give or take a little seasonal fluctuation. Globally, atmospheric levels of CO_2, the most abundant greenhouse gas, are hitting new highs, with no sign yet that the world economic downturn is curbing industrial emissions. Levels of CO_2 are far higher than they've ever been in at least 800,000 years. At their most recent measurements here, CO_2 levels rose to 392 ppm in September, a rise of 2–3 ppm from the same time a year earlier. But of course it's not just CO_2 that is rising. Molecule for molecule, methane is thirty times as potent a greenhouse gas as CO_2. Analysis of Greenland ice cores has established a baseline for atmospheric methane in 1800 of 700 parts per billion (ppb). Ten years ago, when they first measured it on Mount Zeppelin it was 1,850 ppb and today it's even higher. The increase in the amount of CO_2 and methane in the atmosphere is very rapid, 'quite extraordinary actually' one researcher says, looking up from his computer screen. 'We must expect surprises, probably nasty surprises. As humans, we are not invincible.'

23 SEPTEMBER: EAST LOVÉN GLACIER

It has become a familiar comment on my journey, coming up in almost every conversation with people I've met along the way, that the Arctic regions are very responsive to climate change. It's a subject on everyone's lips, whether in relation to melting sea ice, changing weather patterns, or in the movement and vitality of its fauna. But it's only when you have the chance to speak to scientists, and try to understand a little more of their work, that you really begin to appreciate quite how widespread the changes are. One afternoon spent on a glacier, and I realize quite how dynamic, perhaps volatile, the environment has been in the last decade especially.

Since the Little Ice Age, the glaciers of Svalbard have been retreating. In order to understand the response of glaciers in the Kongsfjord area, directly related to weather conditions, scientists here have analyzed measurements taken since the late 1960s. The mean annual temperature has increased by 2°C in forty years and the annual amount of precipitation has also increased some 74 millimetres, with a yearly gradient of +2 millimetres. A little to the south, the meteorological station of Longyearbyen shows an increase of the mean annual temperature of 4°C for the last ninety years.

When they've looked more closely at the wintertime (nine months) and the summertime (three months), they've discovered that the mean increase in the air temperature is more linked to it being less cold in the winter than warmer in the

ABOVE: Learning science from the experts.

summer. In other words, the mean annual air temperature increases more by lack of 'cold' than by excess of 'warm'. The trend in the temperature has consequences on the precipitation, and thus on the glacier's responses. A warm event in winter with pre-cipitation will give rain instead of snow. That may compromise the snow-cover on the glaciers, which can be partially or totally destroyed by rain. Glacier growth and its 'mass-balance' will be therefore negative.

I was able to spend most of today hanging out with one of the French scientific teams. Glaciologist Madeleine Griselin's camp is 5 kilometres away from the main base. Her work including measuring devices with cameras, wind, temperature, pressure, volume and movement, has all helped to formulate a very complex but ever more comprehensible story of glacial formation and loss. Madeleine and her team are very aware that they're just beginning on the journey of discovery, that they've made some very impressive steps, with each piece of information becoming more valuable when pushed up the line to create a greater understanding of our world's ecology as a whole. I was so impressed to see her at work. The Arctic had been her childhood dream, and here she was living it. I asked her a little about her private life. Her reply was sincere:

'How can you be married when you have to pay so much attention to your work?' Indeed, she was married to her work, and I was humbled by this.

It is known that a glacier responds immediately to weather conditions in volume but there is a delay concerning the position of its lowest end, the 'snout'. Again, since the 1960s, scientists here have followed the leading edges, and the surface and volume evolution of many small polar glaciers of the Kongsfjord area, using a combination of direct measurements, aerial photos and GPS data, as technologies have improved. One nearby glacier, the Austre Lovénbreen, has shown significant loss of both surface area and volume. Yet annual variations of air temperature and precipitation do not necessarily give an accurate idea of climate evolution and the glacier response. In the same way, the response of a glacier, often deduced from the position of its snout, does not give any precise information on past climate change. So the glaciologists are also measuring hydrological dynamics, the flux of water and sediments, and all manner of other parameters to try to draw conclusions that might be of use for 'bigger picture' estimates. Our day was finished in French style with a dinner at their camp, with sausages, foie gras and wine. It was a very generous offer to us, from a field team with small budgets that have to go a long way. Out here in the wilderness, each brings a little something of home.

Madeleine's local-scale research is vital to show how climate parameters and a glacier's response might be linked. This is such complicated stuff, and I thought making TV was hard! I've been totally overwhelmed by the passion and dedication of

OPPOSITE: At work on the glacier. I'm not sure what we're doing, but I'm willing to get involved.
BELOW: The glaciers of Svalbard, like many elsewhere in the world, are shrinking, both retreating and reducing in volume.

the scientists here, conducting their intense research on all levels. Many have devoted their careers, their whole lives, to collecting data in this way. We need this sort of commitment, continuity and integrity elsewhere. This is a remarkable place not only for science but for society as a whole.

24 September: Ny-Ålesund

Today was wonderful. Dog sledging, laser beams, polar lights, weather balloons and more. The morning was spent hanging out with a very cool guy, Sebastian from Switzerland, who was one of the managers of the local outpost of the renowned scientific collaborative, the Alfred Wegener Institute for Polar Research. He had been in the Arctic for six years and was loving it. Like Madeleine, it had been a childhood dream to work in this environment, surrounded by such incredible glaciers and snow. There's enough of this for him back home in Switzerland, of course, but the Arctic is something special. He said he'd been bitten by 'Svalbard fever', which many of the people here have caught. I could see why.

I helped release a huge balloon, which was going to measure air pressure, location, temperature and humidity. It had been kept in a warm oven to soften for several weeks and this morning it was filled to about a metre's diameter with helium. The sky was clear, so I sat and watched it as it rose rapidly and lay down to continue to follow it once

I'd put my warm parka jacket on. I watched and watched while everyone else got other shots and chatted. Eventually they couldn't let me stay any longer – the rest of the team were getting impatient. So I knew I had to leave but inside I was reluctant. As Sebastian had said, everyone loves a balloon. I spent another ten minutes watching. Apparently on a good day it would be possible to observe it until it exploded. Simply trailing the speck floating to the heavens – such joy just to release your mind. As it rose, it expanded of course. After ten minutes it was probably as big as the building it had been stored in, Sebastian said, and by the time it exploded it was probably as big as a city office block, a couple of hours and 33 kilometres above sea level later. Now that's cool! The whole thing is tracked by GPS as well as all the data being sent by radio back to the recorder. He showed me a 3D Google Earth display of the track of some previous balloon flights, their readings, and the fall back to the ocean by parachute – I loved it.

Down at sea level, at the foot of Mount Zeppelin, the French are working with the Germans to study the polar stratosphere. So if I got a little excited about the science of a weather balloon, you can imagine how impressed I was when we came back to meet more researchers that night. They're trying to figure out more precisely how clouds are formed, and to analyze their dual reflective and 'blanketing' properties. It's also important to know about the composition, formation, origination, and dispersal of other small particles in the air. These particles, known as aerosols, could be

pollen, spores, water crystals, half combusted carbon from fires and furnaces, and so on. Each water droplet in a cloud has a tiny particle of some sort as its centre and some particles even disperse light without the need for cloud formation. All of this helps us understand better how the sun's rays are reaching the Earth's surface, being reflected back in or away, and hence the influence on global temperatures.

On the roof of one of their buildings is a cluster of remarkable equipment. There's a photometer, which uses the moon as a light source to evaluate the optical depth of these atmospheric aerosols; an infrared spectrometer measures the quantity and type of trace gases. The concentration of ozone in the atmosphere is determined by a laser-radar, which sends its pulse of light 50 times a second into the heavens. To the naked eye, it looks like a solid beam, but those gaps between the pulses are set aside for actually receiving reflected light, measured in thousands of tiny moments, which indicates how high a particle is above the recording station because the speed of light is known – yet this was just the basic stuff.

The German scientist Christian who ran the show was absolutely lovable. He was every bit the eccentric scientist and he sparkled whenever I showed an interest. I loved his enthusiasm and soaked up all I could while the crew sat by waiting for me

to finish. They'd had all they could hack of my ramblings and chatting, so feeling a bit guilty, I left with them. Looking back I wish I'd stayed and absorbed more. Truly it was amazing and added to an overall picture I was gaining of the place – a picture that shone with brilliance, passion and real concern for our planet and a desire to understand it better for all of humankind.

Just as we returned to the boat that we were staying on the northern lights came out to play. We'd half expected them as it was a clear starry night, but the bright full moon meant it was less likely to be a good display than when it is completely dark. But we were wrong. It was a lovely show. Not too fast, but quite a good streak and nice green hue, which matched the laser perfectly that was still beaming up into the night sky. Zubin, our photographer, was beside himself as it was his first sighting; and if lasers, full moon and polar night wasn't enough, he got a shooting star just as they emerged too, such a treat.

The following day, there was yet more remarkable science. I can only give a glimpse of some of the things that were going on during my stay here. I learned about a Norwegian project, 'Cleopatra', that recently showed that climate change here has been affecting the growth conditions of plankton and small crustaceans in the frigid

THE NORTHERN LIGHTS

Perhaps most spectacular of all Arctic phenomena is the *aurora borealis* – the northern lights. Though science, a little prosaically, now tells us they are caused by charged particles of the solar wind interacting with the Earth's magnetic field and colliding with atoms in the upper atmosphere, there is so much still that is perplexing and magical about their appearance. To catch them for the first time, waiting in the cool hush of a polar night, is an experience to be treasured. It's hard not to be moved by what you might see – your patience rewarded whatever the display. Sometimes there is simply a single colour in a thin thread, other nights may reveal cascades of flickering light, green, blue and violet, or folding curtains of magenta and yellow perhaps; veils, arcs and bands, endlessly shifting, fading, burning brightly, then disappearing from view.

In the past it's no surprise that these mystical lights became connected with folk tales and legend. The Sámi spoke of a 'fire fox' racing across the sky, its tail clipping the mountaintops and sending a shower of sparks as it passed. Perhaps, far distant, vast whales were spouting, their jets of breath scattering the light of the stars. For many of the Inuit tribes of Canada the lights signalled the pathway of the recently dead to the heavens, held aloft by ravens. In Greenland, the aurora were the souls of babies who had been lost in childbirth, looking down on a world they never knew, offering love and hope to their parents.

Auroral light is very faint and is now easily overwhelmed by street lighting in northern cities. In years past, sometimes the aurora were seen much further to the south. In Germany, in the sixteenth century, the aurora terrified the country folk who thought they were witness to the wrath of celestial armies, with sparks of light spewing from the thunderous clash of armour and swords. Some Inuit claim to occasionally hear the lights, they describe the faint crackle as the feet of the dead walking across the crisp, fresh snows of heaven. For the Chukchi of Siberia the lights spoke grimly of spirits who had suffered a violent death, the tumble of colours a human skull being kicked around the sky by walruses. All saw the lights as heralding great events or foretelling disasters.

Today, the Arctic remains a place governed by the passage of the seasons and the changing environment. In the popular imagination, and broadly true, the Arctic is a space where for six months of the year the sun shines all day, and for the next six months of the polar winter the land is plunged into darkness, only alleviated perhaps by moonlight and the play of the aurora. While it is true that all places in the Arctic do not see the sun for a period varying from one day at the Circle to half the year at the North Pole itself, the idea of total darkness is not correct. Changes can be both subtle and dramatic. Twilight pervades, light plays tricks. It can be magical, it can distort and disorientate. At times it does feel like another world.

waters. Unicellular algae growing within sea ice, so-called 'ice algae', form the basis of the marine ecosystem. The algae produce essential omega-3 fatty acids, which tiny crustaceans called copepods in turn depend on, and which then carry these fatty acids to the rest of the marine food chain. As a consequence of reduced Arctic sea-ice cover, growth conditions for those tiny organisms change quite dramatically. In particular, light conditions that regulate algal productivity are strongly dependent on ice thickness, structure and precipitation. Researchers have been examining this biomass for many years here and their results are quite clear: algae that were exposed to high light intensities contain lower percentages of omega-3 fatty acids and therefore represent poorer food for grazers. I find it fascinating, and rather worrying, that such small changes can have these huge implications – what might seem small things can have huge consequences.

Another group of scientists has been looking at the movement patterns of ringed seals in the northerly fjords here. Ringed seals are a circumpolar species that are totally dependent on sea ice for all aspects of their life cycle. Ringed seals give birth on ice, they mate, moult and rest on it, and receive considerable protection from it against some predators – particularly killer whales. Just a few months ago, for the very first time, researchers managed to equip a seal here with a new advanced satellite tracker. It is hoped that it will pick up all sorts of information about how these animals live, where they dive and in what oceanographic conditions they feed. This summer was the first field season for this new project, but over a number of years it is hoped that the work will enhance our knowledge of how the seals are coping with the environmental changes, but also to help predict what might happen elsewhere.

There are millions of ringed seals in the Arctic, by far the most common seal species. They eat huge numbers of young fish, cod and herring, and small shrimps and crustaceans. They are themselves preyed upon by Inuit hunters but, far more significantly, they are the single most important prey species for polar bears. Changes in the extent and type of sea ice will certainly have negative impacts on the survival of ringed seals populations, which will in turn have large impacts up and down the Arctic food chain. Some believe changing ice is bringing about a decline in seal reproduction, elsewhere it is believed that the quality and amount of their natural diet is also being altered.

Just a few months before we arrived, a team of more than thirty scientists from various European countries began new work in Ny-Ålesund conducting a large-scale study about the effect of increased CO_2 concentrations on marine life. It is one of a number of EU-funded experiments addressing perhaps one of the most critical topics in the context of ongoing climate change: ocean acidification. Approximately 79 million tons of CO_2 is released into the atmosphere every day – not only as a result of burning fossil fuels, but also the production of cement, deforestation and other changes in land use – and about a third of this gas is absorbed by the world's oceans, which play a key role in helping to moderate climate change. Without this natural ocean capacity, the CO_2 content in the atmosphere would be much higher and global warming and its consequences more dramatic. However, the CO_2 dissolves into seawater and produces a weak acid. It had long been hoped that the oceans were large and inert enough that seawater would not become more acidic. But recent observations now show that the extreme speed of the CO_2 increase caused by man is preventing the oceans from accommodating these changes; the whole of the Earth's oceans are acidifying. Scientists are now quickly trying to work out how animals and plants in the ocean will react to this CO_2 waste. From large predators, through coral reefs and fish stocks, down to bacterial life, which organisms will survive and which will disappear?

It is thought that serious ocean acidification will strike first in the Arctic because of the low temperature of the water. The team brought with them 30 tonnes of equipment, including nine huge floating enclosures (called 'aquatic mesocosms', each of them 17 metres long), transported by ship from Germany. These huge bags were anchored out in the fjord, filled with ambient seawater and then closed by divers. Afterwards, the CO_2 concentration in the seawater was manipulated along a gradient

THIS PAGE: Nearing the end of my visit to Svalbard, I try to find time to reflect on my experiences.

THIS PAGE: In just a few
months the warm glow of
late summer sunlight will
be replaced by the deep
polar winter.

to simulate future concentrations in the ocean. The development of the planktonic and microbial food webs in the bags, together with all kinds of physical and chemical parameters, were followed closely by the scientists. It will take many more months to analyze the data, but one hopes that it will lead to a better understanding of what is happening in this critical area.

At the other end of the globe, Antarctica holds 90 per cent of the world's ice and is the even bigger puzzle in the debate on global warming. Any thawing – a very real risk – could raise sea levels faster than any projections. Even if just a fraction melted, Antarctica could damage nations from Bangladesh and the Maldives to Tuvalu in the Pacific, and cities from New York to Shanghai. There is enough ice, some have calculated, to raise sea levels by a staggering 57 metres if it all melted, over thousands of years. That theoretical possibility would take a very long time, but Antarctica is huge, so even a small change would make a big difference. Yet, scientists are routinely monitoring just a small portion of the continent, maybe as little as 1 per cent.

Most researchers, and insurance companies, are looking at potential sea-level increases and thinking more in terms of a metre. Kim Holmén and the Norwegian Polar Institute have another impressive research base down there, at the Troll Station 250 kilometres in from the coast. Set amid 'jagged mountains like the mythical homes of troll giants', this part of east Antarctica is the 'world's deep freeze' with no sign of a thaw. Temperatures are about minus 15°C even at the height of the Antarctic summer, yet scientists there are wary as we are moving into an era where we are observing changes in the climate system that have never before been seen in human history. Most experts say it is still impossible to model precisely how the ice will react. Our

Earth is dynamic and inherently complicated; that comes as no surprise. Antarctica may actually accumulate more ice this century because of fossil fuel aggravated warming, rather than slide faster into the sea.

Clues to the future emerge in bits and pieces, and 'sometimes in chunks'. In 2002, the floating Larsen B ice shelf fringing the West Antarctica peninsula, a piece of ice the size of Rhode Island, collapsed into the ocean, and the glaciers behind it began dumping land ice into the sea more quickly. Scientists are now watching for the imminent collapse of another peninsular ice shelf, the Wilkins. In 2004 grass began growing on the warming West Antarctica peninsula. Just last year, researchers reported on dramatic biological changes under way: a decline in plankton in the nearby sea, in the krill that feed on it, and in the penguins that feed on the krill. It is clear that Antarctica, like the Arctic, is changing rapidly in unpredictable ways.

Many other ambitious projects were mounted in the just-ended International Polar Year of intensified research. Scientists mapped, via reconnaissance satellite snapshots, the speed with which Antarctica's ice sheets are moving seaward. They sent unmanned mini submarines under the fringing ice shelves to check their status. They drilled 3 kilometres deep into the plateau ice to analyze its chemistry and to read the story of Antarctic climate reaching back 100,000 years. They've even just managed, with a collection of clever instruments and interesting techniques, to enlist and equip lumbering elephant seals to the cause. Their long-distance swims and 300-metre dinnertime dives for squid are giving investigators valuable information about a key piece of the Southern Ocean. The latest analysis of this data confirms that ocean temperatures here are rising faster than the global average.

The core prediction for sea-level rise by the Intergovernmental Panel on Climate Change (the IPCC), which shared the 2007 Nobel Peace Prize with former American Vice-President Al Gore, is for a gain of 18 to 59 centimetres in the coming century, after about 20 centimetres during this past century. This forecast rate included faster ice flow from Antarctica and Greenland observed in a ten-year period from 1993, but the IPCC says this could increase or decrease in the future. If the flow grows in line with temperature rises, it would add a further 10–20 centimetres. But, the fundamental problem really is that this predicted range only takes into account things that can be modelled. There are other scenarios that suggest it is plausible to say there will be much larger changes. One worrying possibility is the chance Antarctica will slide faster into the sea, perhaps it's ring of sea ice melting away in warmer oceans. Or, meltwater might increase under the ice sheets, acting as a lubricant and speeding a slide. In the long term, whatever the precise nature of the change, we are surely in trouble. Some are now suggesting Greenland is also close to a 'tipping point', an irreversible meltdown that could last a number of centuries. Worst-case scenario – if it all vanished – is that Greenland has enough ice to raise world sea levels by 7 metres.

26 September: Longyearbyen

Back in town, I finally managed to meet up with Swedish Professor Kim Holmén, the Research Director of the Norwegian Polar Institute based in Tromsø, after hearing so much about his wonderful work. A reputation for a unique style also precedes him.

He wears dark sunglasses and a long, grey-white beard. He looks a little like an ageing rocker, perhaps the guitarist from ZZ Top. It's been said to him before. He was out late at a birthday party last night, but he's lively and full of facts, a real pro. The beard, he told me, had grown out of a bet he'd made with a guy working up at Ny-Ålesund ten years ago over who could grow the longest. 'Who won?' I asked Kim as a way of breaking the ice. 'Nobody yet,' he said with a smile, stroking his beard. We try to find a good place to shoot an interview outside, in the fast disappearing sun, and he takes our faffing in his stride. I pull my collar up to the cool breeze. I wouldn't mind a beard right now.

I talked at length with Kim about his research and his feelings for the future. The 54-year-old has become a leading scientific spokesperson as well being at the top of his field, the atmospheric sciences. His mentor at university was Bert Bolin, a giant in the field of meteorology, who was one of the first scientists to alert the world to the threats of climate change. Bolin was head of the World Climate Research Programme and the first chairman of the IPCC, winning the Nobel prize with Gore. Despite such accolades, Bolin remained humble to his dying days. 'I remember asking him once how many great ideas he came up with during his long career,' the equally modest Holmén recalls. 'He thought about this for a moment and then said "three and a half".'

No one person is going to come up with the answer to solve all of the world's concerns, of course, but men like Bolin, and Holmén in his own way, are fine examples of what brilliant work can and must be done. As an early question in our

OPPOSITE: Now back in the Russian Arctic we are greeted by a chilly dawn.

interview, knowingly, I asked about the 'speculation' that humans are to cause for climate change. His response was quick and his answer full: 'I dislike the word speculation Bruce. We know that CO_2 is increasing in the atmosphere, we know that it's because of mankind, and we also know the physics much better now; simply, that if you increase greenhouse gases, something must get warmer. Climate has always changed, will always change, and one of the difficulties with climate debate is that people mix timescales. We have changes on long timescales, short timescales. The changes that we see now are quite rapid, and I would argue that some of the changes we are experiencing are much more rapid than we find in the historical records and they're difficult to accommodate within the span of natural variability. Part of the signal is natural but part of it is undoubtedly human induced. In the Arctic the evidence is clear to see. The winters will continue to freeze over for quite a long time, certainly in the foreseeable future, but the Arctic will become less and less ice covered during the summer months.'

Why then is there such a bitter debate about climate change, I ask? Why are there so many sceptics or those who are so fatalistic and say, 'there's nothing we can do?' 'Well, I can't speak for other people,' Kim replied, 'but there are many things at stake here. It is something that touches us all, because we might have to change things unwillingly, and so people are right to question that. And before we take such decisions in our daily life we might want to be sure we are doing something good.' I explain that I feel the same frustrations. 'As climate researchers,' he continued, 'we are often criticized that we don't know the exact answers. Certainly, the flip side of that is we also don't know exactly how bad the problems are, and so we all must have a responsibility of being careful when we don't know for sure what the impacts of a particular action, or development, might be.' The changes the globe is experiencing are because of you, me and everyone else, I agree, so it must come down to responsibility at the individual level? 'Yes Bruce, but society must also provide opportunities for good choices,' he said. 'We mustn't moralize about our individual lives unless society, and here I mean government and our culture, actually provides good choices for us. But we cannot hide and say that's somebody else's business. It's all of our business; this affects all of us.'

It was refreshing to hear this sort of honest, straightforward talk from such a leading man of science. Kim's work, and that of his colleagues, is revealing to us many of the intricate causes for climate change, but there is still so much to learn and understand, so much complexity to unravel. Do we just wait till there are more definitive answers, or should we not be trying to do everything we can to help now, I ask? 'We are often faced with having to make decisions without knowing everything and we must build knowledge as best we can based on the models of today and the data that we have collected today. And we must trust that these scientists have done a solid and honest job, which I do believe all of them are doing, working hard, harder than many, to produce as good results as they can. And with that trust we must make some decisions today, because if we wait and wait and wait then we are in a situation that is even more difficult to remedy if it turns out to be as difficult as it could be.'

Another aspect I've long felt is an issue, is that so many of those nations that are polluting the most really should also be capable of helping the most. But, at present they are not, and they are putting restrictions on the developing world, without putting their own house in order. Kim is a great diplomat, and his replies to my doubts were convincing. 'The same countries that could be doing the most are doing less than they could in some of the structural changes we must have in the energy system, I agree, but they are also contributing the most to the research that actually lets us know what is going on. So the world is not black and white. You have to acknowledge that North America, Europe, Japan, are very strong on climate change research and are also providing the vital information that we need to better inform our way forward. For our own part in this process, Ny-Ålesund is both a fantastic place and a great idea – to collect many different disciplines and many different nationalities in one single place to research together. Culturally and scientifically this is the challenge to point us in directions where we can do good things together to increase knowledge for mankind'.

Kim shakes my hand as I leave. 'It's actually all very simple,' he says. 'I believe in humanity. I believe in humans. It will be hard work for all us but if I look at the discussions about climate change and man-made impacts on the environment in the past thirty years, there has been a movement of hope to make something happen. I do believe that when more people understand and see what is happening, and if we can

OPPOSITE: After a long journey by rail and dirt track, we reach the village of Nyukhcha.
BELOW: I'd love one of these trucks for the rough roads of Ibiza back home.

present trustworthy and solid science, then we can make a serious impression on people. To give you one final example, I'm inspired by what has happened with smoking in restaurants. I know it's not the same, but it's a question of human willingness to push for change. Forty years ago it would have been politically impossible to discuss banning smoking, but after many years of discussion and information it suddenly was quite simple to take that step. And the benefits of this are huge to so many people. It seems obvious doesn't it?'

29 SEPTEMBER: MURMANSK

Russian border control is an absolute nightmare. Everyone always jokes about it – maybe it's become something of the travel writer's cliché, to talk about how much of a pain it is to fight the red tape here. Usually you hear stories of officious uniformed officers, days spent holed up in plastic-chaired passport offices, stale cigarette smoke, endless stamping of papers, orders barked and little humour. Well, in my experience, travelling through Russia as a film crew always has its moments, and our return here was no exception.

We took the chance of a flight from Tromsø to Archangelsk, but we had to land and clear customs in Murmansk en route. We'd lugged our forty-odd boxes of camera gear and film from plane to plane, and now through a crowded airport. Each load took many hours, but at Murmansk another spanner was thrown into the works. The Russian border guards evidently wanted to give us as much hassle as possible, and we spent the best part of a whole day having to jump through their hoops. Every single bag, every

single piece of kit was unloaded and checked, logged, inventoried, tagged and photographed. Such a long process. At times, I think it's easier to count a herd of reindeer.

30 September: Arkhangelsk

I'm in the city of Arkhangelsk, on the shores of the White Sea. The buildings are as square and concrete as in eastern Russia, the cars as grey and utilitarian. Yesterday we flew in from Murmansk and later today we will catch a train for a six-hour journey to hang out with an ex-KGB agent who used to work in Vietnam and now lives in the boreal forest as therapy for his post traumatic stress disorder. This is all very recent as a storyline, as we were going to film with the Russian military, maybe on a submarine or a nuclear icebreaker but our permits were denied at the eleventh hour.

The railroad was straight and flat and we passed a few towns and villages at first, but their number dwindled as we escaped the urban sprawl. Unloading at Karpogory, we bundle our mountain of gear into another convoy of beaten up old campervans and hit the road. Trees line our route the whole way, like driving down a narrow corridor. We fix a puncture in the mud somewhere as snow begins to fall. I drift in and out of sleep.

We arrive about 4 a.m. Our digs in the tiny village of Nyukhcha are two wooden huts blanketed with linoleum and 1960s wallpaper, single iron beds, and a small wood-burning stove, which took the room from frozen to t-shirt comfortable in just

half an hour. Apparently we're the first foreigners to stay here. We sat and ate some local bread and cheese, then gave in to our tiredness and crashed.

Next day we make our way to the village hall where about thirty women in shawls and a couple of men are waiting for us. Today is the International Day of the Elderly – or Pensioners' Day – and although it's a UN date, I'd never known it celebrated elsewhere. But here it was being taken on with gusto. We sat and shared potato salad, tomatoes and coleslaw, soup and sausages. A man made the rounds with his piano-accordion. Little old ladies were pouring vodka into each other's cups of tea while their friends weren't looking. It was instantly a fun scene, everyone was happy and chatting, and what transpired was a morning of great celebration, songs, dances, poetry and sketches, and not forgetting lots of toasts too.

In Soviet times there was a state farm logging enterprise here, but before the Revolution the place was fiercely independent. People moved here to avoid taxes or sending their sons off to the Tsar's army. Others, it seems, came here to hide. Nowadays there is vast private logging concession, yet huge local unemployment. Most of the young are leaving the forests to seek education and jobs in the cities, but the elderly remain proud of their place in the world, certainly if today was anything to go by. Some spoke with nostalgia of the days when everything was organized for you, others said it was a lot of work with little reward.

4 OCTOBER: NYUKHCHA

I've been in this community now for a few days and our filming is going well, but I don't know how much will make our final cut. After the old peoples' festival we spent the next days out with our central characters, Alexei Ivanovich and Katya. Alexei is the head of the forestry and hunting for the area. An ex-KGB operative from the jungles of Cambodia and Vietnam, he's in love with the woods. He talks to the trees and feels a real connection with them. He sees the forest as spiritually alive. I love him for this and agree.

We get on well but our conversations falter when I question him about poor regulation and corruption. He becomes quiet, or repeats the same phrases robotically, like reading from a script. Lenin called the forests 'the green money', and the forest here is still worth billions. But, according to some studies, it's estimated that 90 per cent of trade from Russia is illegal and as Russia is the world's largest exporter of round wood – whole logs and trees – it makes it hard to trace as it all gets processed abroad and mixed with legitimate wood. Most of the corruption occurs through legitimate trade routes and tax evasion, but illegal wood disguised as legal timber is truly a worry. Power is in the hands of the oligarchs and organized crime networks.

Alexei says that such problems haven't reached this part of Russia. It's hard for me to question him further on this subject because he's the boss here and any insight would be an admission of his own guilt. He says the roads are not good enough and the locals would hear about it and not stand for it, but he evades my questions. Our translator says that she lost her cousin through mafia murder as a direct result of dealing with the illegal timber barons in this area, so maybe Alexei is just protecting his family. Maybe he's involved, maybe not? It's so hard to tell and who am I to come here and ask such questions. Times are hard – if it's not corrupt Soviet officials having a good life off the masses it's now the corporations. Not much has changed in a way. Many will soak their days with vodka, buying it with their parents' pension. Life is tough here, that's for sure.

Everyone keeps a vegetable garden and gathers from the woods, but it's hard to be totally independent. They can't even collect their own firewood from the forest. Everything is state controlled and the chopping of a tree will result, at least in principle, in a

OPPOSITE: I'm taken into the woods, where Alexei and I discuss the health of the forest. BELOW: The deforested areas are shocking to behold but they are slowly being replanted.

three-to-seven year imprisonment. Hunting is allowed but again with strict regulation and paperwork. Bureaucracy is very much part of the system and everyone seems to accept it. It is frustrating to think some timber baron is making millions, harvesting the forest that these people have lived with forever but now cannot cut for themselves.

Katya is a very different character, a wonderful lady of about 60 who has eleven grandchildren. Her husband died of cancer a few years ago, and now she lives alone in a small house set apart at the edge of the forest. She goes out every day to forage, with her mushroom basket, metal knapsack and a samovar full of snacks. 'The trees really are life for me, even though everyone thinks I'm a witch,' she tells me as I join her. We make our way along a small muddy track, deep into the woods.

The forest may look quite monotonous at first sight but it's a glorious chaos inside. Huge swathes of old-growth fir, dense clumps of larch and birch, mossy swamps and open glades. Some places are so ancient that the lichen sticks up like pale white bonsai trees. Moss covers trunks and branches like old men's beards. The woodland, the *taiga*, is magical to be in and when you stop for a moment it's completely silent. The trees go on for hundreds, maybe thousands, of miles. It's one of the biggest ecosystems on Earth. They are absolute bliss to be in and I've loved my time here.

We spent whole days collecting mushrooms and moss and searching desperately for berries. There are dozens of varieties, each with their own seasons, but all are in short supply this year. It's the main topic of discussion with everyone we've met. Only the oily-head or buttery-head mushrooms are here in any number, on grassy verges and underneath rotting clumps. Katya kept saying that this area would usually be covered in this or that berry but instead, like last year, the forest is empty. She didn't know what to put this down to but suggested everything went in seasons and cycles and this was just another cycle, perhaps another bad year. She wasn't overly worried but did say that she could detect that things were warmer, for sure. At one point she said that a particular berry had completely gone because the birds had got them all, birds which didn't usually come here but had arrived because of terrible fires in the south of Russia.

Alexei repeated this story too, but no one was particularly willing to suggest the cause. Alexei had read many Russian scientific papers and believed in climate change, but he didn't know if this was the reason why his spruce was dying – which it was. Alexei took me to an area of complete deforestation. It looked desperate, like an apocalypse, but then I was expecting that. The area had been completely clear-felled because the trees had been dying. Some trees had been left, and replanting was taking place across the whole area but it was never going to look anything other than horrific to my eyes. We also looked at a place of beautiful old-growth trees. Here there was little vegetation on the ground but, just like in the rain forest, everything was much denser at the canopy level. It was stunningly beautiful.

Katya took me fishing for sprats with a net curtain on poles. She'd also found an

OPPOSITE: Katya, my guide to the forest. We foraged for berries and elusive mushrooms, and I loved every minute of it.

BELOW: Katya takes me to a
nearby river to catch our lunch.
OPPOSITE: Despite the tough
way of life here, there is still
hope and laughter. I treasure
my time with her.

Amanita mushroom, the fly agaric toadstool famed for its hallucinogens, which we chopped into a bottle for turning into oil. I helped to dig her garden and used the moss we'd collected to fill gaps in the sides of her log cabin for insulation. The birds, she says, will steal it back in the spring for their nests. While in the garden she shed a tear, telling me how lonely she was after her children had gone and her husband had died. Yet, she had made a mental decision to be happy and she looked to the forest as her friend. Many years ago she could hardly walk and it was the forest, she tells me, that had cured her. She found the energy to move and, a little more each day, she went deeper into the woods. She rubs a potion of fly agaric on her knees and hands when they are sore, especially in the later winter, and finds this gives her the strength to continue her journeys in the woods.

6 OCTOBER: NYUKHCHA

Today I joined Ivan to collect fodder for his livestock, so we coupled his horse and cart and headed out to the hayfields. All the farm apparatus here is pretty antique, there are a few tractors around and about, mostly ancient, a few sidecar motorbikes too, but much of the work is done with horses. I've seen ploughs, potato-diggers, hay-collectors and straw-cutters, all horse drawn, and an amazing array of wonderful old rusty ironwork in shapes that boggle the imagination.

At the edge of the village, we passed the derelict buildings of the old state farm. Ivan remembers working here as a boy with the whole village, and he recalls it fondly.

The local community tried to keep the state farm going as a cooperative for many years after the collapse of the Soviet Union – under different guises and with different names – but ten years later it was finally closed down and now lies in ruins. Ivan said that the problem was the lack of an assured marketplace. His answers all felt very genuine and from the heart, different to those of Alexei who was more prone to toe the party line. Ivan said that some people lamented the old days, there was a certain comfort in knowing that you were being looked after in some way, no matter what – or seemingly no matter what – and even though life was tough and work was hard you knew you could survive. All feel the insecurity of life today, where there was real fear of the future and one's place in it. What I found curious was the fact that people are making millions from this forest while he will be arrested if he chops one tree. What was that all about? He agreed that this didn't seem right and is confused by it all.

We shared lunch back at his house, where I met his beautiful wife and their young daughter. Their eldest daughter is 19 and at college, training to be a tax clerk, and their son is away at a secondary school, weekly boarding. Their daughter is waiting to get into university, which she will attend for free if she passes some exams,

ABOVE: Collecting fodder for the horses with Ivan as winter approaches.

or with cost if she doesn't. I didn't ask if they could afford it if she failed. Ivan and his wife now spend most of each day caring for his father, who is deaf, blind, and had lost both his legs from diabetes. Their circumstances are difficult, but judging by Ivan's level of intelligence they could easily be making a living elsewhere. They are content and want to continue life as they are. They tell me they enjoy their life with the forest and don't want to put their father into care.

On my last full day Alexei took us all to a place where his favourite tree, the cedar, was growing strong after being planted twenty years ago. He also brought some saplings along for us to plant together. Around us, other saplings of a few years growth were just ankle high, and it reminded me how slowly everything grows here in the North. This particular area will look desolate for many years to come. We continued on to another spot in the forest, where other trees looked healthy and strong. It reminded me of my youth, my schoolhouse was called Cedars and had a collection of massive ancient trees in its gardens. On our trek into this particular patch we also came across a huge clump of fly agaric, which I eagerly gathered up for Katya. We later filled two bottles of magic potion, which I hope won't explode in my bag on the way home.

James, my director, asked me to give a conclusion to this short episode in our film, while we were standing in the woods, so together we hastily scripted a few lines. I tried to mix talk of corruption, climate change and love of the forests, but it will always be a sound bite version of what I really think. We finished the day with a *shash-lik* – pork kebabs – that Alexei had been longing to have with us since our arrival. The location was a dreamy spot: a hayfield created in an open glade in an endless wood-land. Nearby was a small river with fish jumping, and the smoke of our small fire drifted slowly toward it. It was here also that Alexei finally told me of the horrors of his past, about his time in the KGB fighting in Kampuchea and Vietnam. He'd seen things that had shocked him so deeply that he suffered from nightmares for many years. The day of his retirement from the military he came back to the *taiga* and walked alone into the forests. The next years were to be his therapy. It was an over-whelming force of nature that had helped him to find peace for his troubled mind. This was why he loved the forest so much and I had to agree with him.

19 OCTOBER: TØNSVIK

Up north in Norway, sat in a *lavvu* tent in the pissing rain. It's been over a week since I last had time to write my diary. So much has happened, but I'm due out to join the herders so I will have to sum it all up quickly.

I'm living with a group of Sámi, the Oskal family. The herd was started by four brothers who came to the area in the 1950s after the area was vacated following the war. There are over 40,000 Sámi in northern Norway, and many more in other Scan-dinavian countries. Once reindeer herders and fishermen, most are now town dwellers and only a tiny minority still stay with the deer year round, living solely from the land. They have all been marginalized and persecuted in time, though compared to the North American indigenous peoples their treatment has been relatively benign. Their story here is particularly interesting because this particular Sámi family face an increasing number of pressures from the urban centre Tromsø, just 20 kilo-metres away from where we're camped. Unsurprisingly, it has had a real impact on their lives and culture.

The homeland of the Sámi has always been rich in natural resources. At different times in its history, this area 'Sápmi' has been a hub of trade and human contact. It has been an ongoing story of changes in culture and society. Sápmi has never been an unexplored virgin wilderness. It has always been, and continues to be, the home of the Sámi people.

I'd connected with some of the young herders when I'd passed through town on my way to Russia earlier in the month. I'd spent a day out on the hill with Johan Isak and Danel Oskal, both energetic men with infectious laughs. We'd chased the herd around the mountainside for a good few hours, alternatively sprinting to cut them off, hiding behind rocky outcrops while others ushered them past us or waiting for the crew to catch up. Often the climbs were steep and relentless, poor Zubin and cameraman Richard worked so hard, with all their heavy equipment, 8 kilograms of

ABOVE: The glades are bathed in dappled sunlight. There is immense beauty in the Russian taiga.

OPPOSITE LEFT: At last we found it – the Amanita mushroom, famous in fairy tales and now destined for one of Katya's potions.

OPPOSITE RIGHT: The last supper, with pork kebabs and a toast to my hosts.

metal strapped to their chests. All around us, in broken mist, the views were tantalizing: tall mountains, deep valleys, heathland and fjord, and on ridges in all directions, scattered groups of reindeer.

After some time, we returned to a sheltered grassy patch, where we got a primus stove out and shared a meal of reindeer meat and heart. I asked about the food. 'Healthy fat in reindeer,' Johan said proudly, 'much better than pork and beef from the supermarket.' This was true, but said while emptying his tub of cream – crème fraiche – onto it with a smile. 'But we like modern fats too.' No fool, he has a foot in both worlds and knows what he likes of each.

It's not always been an easy time though. Throughout much of the nineteenth century the Sámi were thought to pose a threat to Norway's interests in the North because they were perceived as alien, primitive, fundamentally 'un-Norwegian'. The church and the school system sought to assimilate, to eradicate difference. Today, thankfully, much is different. The Sámi are recognized as a unique people. They are entitled to their own language, to speak as a people on the national stage and, to a certain degree, be heard as a people. They are still far from being an equal partner, but new possibilities for partnerships are emerging. The times are changing again, and with the growing demands for oil, gas and minerals, and for transportation thoroughfares through their homeland, the Sámi will have to be as adaptable as their ancestors to survive with their culture and identity intact.

The family I'm working with has been fighting a number of battles against the encroachment of more dominant cultures. They'd recently had a protracted battle with the Norwegian military and NATO over live-firing training areas in their lands. They had lost. The military had also wanted to build a road through their grazing lands, which the herders said would cause great disruption to the welfare of the herd. Again, their voices had not won out, although they had been financially compensated. A fight they had recently won, against the whole of Norway it seems, was over proposals to host the Winter Olympics in Tromsø which would have meant the development of much of the local area, including the Sámi's sacred mountain. The whole debate had been fought in the courts and with an unforgiving media, which had resulted in a fair bit of demonizing of the Sámi people. For them it was a PR disaster, but from their perspective what could they do? It was capitulate and end thousands of years of tradition and lifestyle or fight. They had no choice.

On many days we were stuck in our *lavvu*, or in a refuge hut out on the hill, unable to go anywhere because of the awful conditions. It has been snowing solidly now for four days. Once or twice we had tried to go out on motorbikes and snow-machines, but it was such hard work. My battered old machine kept diving into riverbeds, lurching

against boulders and coming to a grinding stop. At other times the light played tricks on us, sometimes so diffuse that there was no shadow, no definition and it was hard to discern land from sky. The whiteouts held us inside a ball of freezing snow and fog.

On the morning of the sixth day the snow was now so deep there was no point going out at all, pointless if you can't see where the deer are. Even if you can round up a few, there's no point because you'll only have to come back to get the rest. So if they can't see them on the hills they just don't bother going up. But this was the main issue in modern times, they can no longer just wait for the weather to improve. Previously they used to migrate with the deer around the fjord to their winter pastures, but now the area is so built up with so many houses that they just can't do it. And so Danel's grandfather, thirty years ago, had written a letter to the King of Norway asking if they could use a boat, because it was proving impossible for them to move their deer through the morass of houses. The King lent them a military boat, which has been used ever since.

A generous gesture, and now an essential tool, but for the Sámi it was still a reluctant concession to change. In years past, they moved when the deer moved. And that meant that they just had a philosophical approach to things that was relatively stress-free. You can't get upset that the weather's bad, because that's not going to help anything. And so because it's much bigger than you, and you can't control it, you learn to just be with it. And so that's why they're all a very pragmatic, matter-of-fact people. However, suddenly having a date in the diary to make the boat – a boat that wouldn't wait for them because it also serves a number of other herds up and down the fjords – was causing real anxiety. If they didn't meet the deadline they had to find other means of getting their animals to the winter pasture, which in essence meant a lot more stress on their animals and a lot more stress on them. Huge expense, complicated logistics, hundreds of truck journeys, endless separation of groups within the herd – a real nightmare.

So, this was the plan. All of our different teams, out on snow machines and quad bikes, were trying to bring groups together into big herds and then down whichever routes they could. All knew the deer had certain paths that they enjoyed taking off the hills, but they now had to try to push them into the most incongruous of places that deer would never usually go through: past houses, across roads, between telegraph poles, and using a whole bunch of modern machinery into a large corral and paddock, to wait for the arrival of the boat. And, after almost a week of patience, and implausibly hard work, we did it. We even used a helicopter to spot the last isolated groups and then to try and rush the mass down a major valley to get to the beach in time.

20 October: Tønsvik

One final day of lassoing animals in the mud and marking their ears. Johan and Danel's girlfriends have come to join us and help out. Danel's gentle and thoroughly modern Sámi sister also came. She's studying at university, actively trying to equip herself in science and a language of politics that could benefit her family in their struggle in the years ahead. To everyone's relief the boat is late – the crew had a day off over the weekend and were in Tromsø getting drunk. It's a little hilarious, but also wonderful news for us as we've still so much to do.

All the animals have been put in a big paddock and observed. We lasso every animal that doesn't have an earmark, mostly the first-year calves and on those animals we then put a large tag around their necks with a number on it. Once you chase around trying to lasso animals it's very hard to identify which calves are suckling with which mothers. We go and have lunch, and by the time we've returned the animals and their young have paired up once more. A few more hours with notepad and paper tallying up all the numbers and logging mothers and calves. You could then see who owned which. Once everyone had made their own lists, all the numbers were brought together, corroborated, checked, debated a little, and then settled with a consensus. Any discrepancies were checked once again, they'd go back to the corral to have another look and make sure that everyone was happy.

Once everyone was in agreement, we returned to encourage the animals through the corral down a series of fenced routes. Tags were removed and other reindeer were re-marked. Some people, including Johan Isak's girlfriend, were measuring the animals for a scientific study; a few were given GPS collars. Others were being injected with compounds in an effort to rid them of the troublesome warble fly, the scourge of the caribou in Canada too. All the different Sámi families come together at this stage to attend to the herd's health. A small group of unlucky reindeer were heading off for slaughter, while the main group was led down into another enclosure, ready for their journey to the winter pastures.

On the final day, we forced the animals down to the beach, across a small road, and into the water. There was the boat now waiting for them – a naval landing craft, in fact – with it's bow gaping open, and a ramp lowered, ready for the passengers to come onboard. After an hour of rushing hooves, bellowed orders, splashes and shouts, nearly a thousand reindeer are afloat.

As I stand on that boat, heading down the fjord, naturally I think more about what the future holds for this amazing Arctic place. It's hard to juggle all the information in my head. It's been such an incredible journey. A few weeks later, back in the UK, we listen again to my interview with Kim Holmén, a genius really and so generous with his time. 'Well, the Arctic will continue to change,' he had told me simply. 'Certainly, we see from our models that the Arctic is a very sensitive area and many of the hardships you have seen on your travels will continue and become even tougher. Most of the species that are dependent on this environment will struggle, but life also goes on without them, even though that will be very sad. There are few of us that have the privilege of seeing a wild polar bear, out in it's own habitat, but I think many more would feel that the world is poorer if we lose animals like this. However, changes in the Arctic also spread out into the world causing disruption elsewhere. In China a few months ago we had discussions about how a changing Arctic influences the rain over their country. It's quite clear that there are similar couplings extending elsewhere in the world. So the change in the Arctic is not only for the polar bears or the reindeer, not only for the people that live here, but it is also important for much of the rest of the world. And that is certainly serious.'

Some of these changes are global, vast and complex, and seemingly out of reach. Others, like those facing my Sámi friends are very obvious. The boat I'm standing on is itself an indication of how, even unwittingly, a modern piece of transport presents a major disruption in their world – an arbitrary, expensive, immovable date in the diary – and the stress that this brings to their lifestyles and the health of their animals.

The traditional way of life here, the connection they have with the animals and their landscape is not just physical, nor is it imaginary. It is a set of values, a different way of seeing the world, a spirituality perhaps. A series of encroachments, sometimes

OPPOSITE: In the final push, the weather clears and a helicopter is used to drive the last groups down the valley.

gradual, sometimes immediate, with the schooling, the forced assimilation, the urban sprawl, the urban way of thinking, isn't just changing their lifestyle though, it's affecting the ways they are able to interact with each other. This, I believe, is why it's important to listen to them before that value system erodes completely.

It's this respect for the land, a way of living within one's environment, that really is likely to disappear completely for many peoples of the North in the next generation. It would be much more than just a shame if this were to be lost – it would be a tragedy. During my time in the North I've certainly experienced a way of interaction that is more respectful, perhaps more humanly innate, than I see elsewhere. It's the simple idea of more cooperation and less competition, more sharing and less greed, a respect for all life. After all my travels, I see a clear message in this. The many communities here offer us a way to think more about what it is to be human. It's a lesson that, at this time in our planet's history, is more important than ever.

THESE PAGES: My travels are at an end, floating on a landing craft on our way to the winter pastures.
OVERLEAF: The modern Arctic is a dynamic place that still has the power to inspire.

A POLE OF PEACE? When Gorbachev made a famous speech in Murmansk in 1987 heralding the end of the Cold War, he predicted a new era of cooperation and peace in the Arctic. Environmental protection strategies were tabled, international agreements proposed and, by 1996, an Arctic Council was formed. The Council, however, remains a 'soft law institution': it advises, oversees research, and provides a forum for indigenous voices. It does not consider military matters, and while the Cold War may be over, the USA and Russia still have their submarines patrolling under the Arctic Ocean. The political and environmental landscape is dynamic and has changed dramatically in recent years. Now, as each day passes, new voices add to the chorus of disquiet about what is happening, and what should be done – whether over energy resources, new shipping routes, fisheries, security concerns, and all manner of environmental perils. Will there be a new 'great game', a polar 'land rush'? Are we facing a cataclysmic 'northern meltdown'? Though it would be overblown to predict impending geopolitical disorder, without consensus and coherence there is so much to be gained, and to be lost, in the modern Arctic.

Such scenarios may be remotely possible, but they are not inevitable. With rising tensions over maritime claims and growing alarm over the environmental consequences and industrial opportunities of climate change, the Arctic now must be at the centre of issues for international agreement. In 2008 the US Geological Survey estimated that 90 billion barrels of undiscovered but technically recoverable oil exists north of the Arctic Circle. Other reports tantalize with promises of some 50 trillion cubic metres of natural gas. However impressive these figures first were, they now seem to increase all the time, with new estimates in the press varying wildly. With vast tracts of open water appearing, the door is beginning to open to new oil and gas fields and new fisheries. The Northeast and Northwest Passages may also soon become navigable on an annual basis. There is even talk in some circles of a possible sea route right over the Pole between the Atlantic and the Pacific, which no doubt could have important implications for trade with China. These are speculations of the past that may soon become real possibilities as our planet warms.

But it is the pursuit of oil that drives the bubbling international tensions in the region, as first the Russians,

then the Norwegians, and soon the Canadians, Danes and the Americans stake their overlapping claims to the Arctic seabed. All of these developments place a spotlight on how the Arctic is being managed and whether countries with vested interests in the region are capable of dealing with these new challenges in a responsible way, thinking beyond their own ambitions and borders. It may indeed be time for the Arctic Council to evolve to meet its emerging needs. There may also be call for a new Arctic Treaty, a regime of guiding principles to include respect for the environment, the sustainable management of natural resources, the freedom of scientific research, and the long-overdue involvement of indigenous peoples in a meaningful way, and an acknowledgement of their rights. This treaty would only be a starting point, but it may make it possible to move from words to positive action. Cooperation, not conflict, must be the guiding light but can the interests of individual nations be satisfied for the lasting benefit of all?

Epilogue
A GATHERING STORM?

My travels in the Arctic are at an end, just one tiny journey among hundreds of thousands that are made here with every turn of the tide, or the passing of each day. Through forest, across tundra and over ice floe, animals and humans are constantly on the move in this dynamic, magical, and increasingly modern part of our planet.

For hundreds of years, the Arctic has been viewed as a place on top of the world but at the margins of human activity; a timeless region where one might delight, momentarily, at the beauty of a cathedral-like iceberg before being overtaken by penetrating, life-sapping coldness. It was a place best enjoyed, if at all, in the pages of a book, and from the warmth of an armchair. It was a place that would take its dreadful toll on a roll-call of explorers, many who never returned from its icy embrace. In time, the Far North came to be viewed with contempt, its people backward and the land a barren wilderness without promise, good for nothing much more than science and extravagant hunting trips. In today's world, however, views like these are shrinking, like the ice. The region is now fated to become the testing site, the battleground perhaps, for many vital twenty-first century concerns.

Part of the Arctic's attraction, I suppose — and its mystery — is that it has for so long been a land of silence, seemingly out of reach. 'Have you ever stood where the silences brood, and vast the horizons begin', asked Robert Service in his poem 'The Land of Beyond'. One of the last places on Earth to be disturbed by humans, it's an environment that has always challenged the abilities of people, animals and plants to survive and flourish. Though there may be something innate within us to desire the freedom

THIS PAGE: What does the future hold for the hunters of the High Arctic?

and the emptiness of the wilds, there is now no room for nostalgia or sentimentality. My own preconceptions of the Arctic have matured hugely in these past seven months. The Arctic is no longer a land beyond the attention and ambitions of man; it is no longer an untouched wilderness set apart from the rest of the world. I believe much of our future history will be written here.

I've travelled with Greenlandic hunters and Siberian herders, listened to their fears for the future and tried to understand a little more about their connection to the past. I have joined the crew of a commercial fishing boat and seen the riches they have taken from our ocean. I have encountered whalers, bureaucrats, geologists and gold-diggers, all taking their share of the bounty available here. I have met scientists who have explained their findings to me. I have searched for the wild Arctic caribou and reindeer and have come to appreciate just how important these species are for north-erners worldwide, especially for the nutritional, cultural and spiritual needs of indigenous peoples. I sit with my companions on soft turf in the pouring rain and share whispered words of hope.

The North Pole is being transformed from a sea-ice cap to a seasonally ice-free sea. With the diminishing ice cover, there is new global interest in the extensive energy, shipping, fishing and tourism prospects in the Arctic Ocean. I have learned how a number of countries, including the major Arctic powers, are increasingly asserting their sovereignty seawards. Russia is not alone as a nuclear-capable state adjusting its strategic deployments in the Arctic Ocean. There are forums for interna-tional co-operation here, most notably the Arctic Council, but peace in the Arctic has yet to be explicitly established as the guiding light for a common interest.

The Arctic is now considered the next frontier of hydrocarbon exploration, and although the environmental risks are high, the world's superpowers are eyeing up the region's riches. The image of a future ice-free Arctic Ocean and the prospects of polar bears and Inuit peoples struggling in the Far North are at odds with how people per-ceive this land, and it provokes scientific and public anxiety. Just how long this anxiety will delay development here is not certain.

The age of 'easy oil' is over and despite the catastrophic spill in the Gulf of Mexico the oil industry is still aiming to secure deepwater reserves in unconven-tional and extreme locations. Geologists have identified the Arctic basin as likely to hold vast oil and gas reserves. From the Beaufort to the Barents Sea, even offshore West Greenland, the process of exploration has begun. Yet, global energy demand shows no sign of slowing down. And until renewable alternatives are economically viable, and more widely available, it is still necessary to look for oil here. But this means yet more greenhouse gas emissions, more environmental damage, more money spent on every litre of oil produced, and more cost for every kilometre trav-elled in our cars. In my view the drive to extract more resources in the Arctic will

OPPOSITE: A chunk of ice rests at the water's edge in a fjord in Svalbard.

forever change one of the very last, near pristine areas of this planet. And there will be no going back.

If I close my eyes and search inside my heart for what has affected me most these past months it's the voices of the indigenous peoples that have spoken to me more clearly than any others. I hear their concerns and frustrations at the speed of change in the North and begin to recognize how modernity has disconnected them from their land and traditions. Of course, change brings new opportunities, but in many places it feels as though something has been severed: a mindset, a spiritual belief, an ethos, a moral code perhaps?

I believe that all of us must, once again, rediscover our spiritual connection to Mother Earth. I am aware of how strange this may sound, but it is my firm belief, having learned so much from the wisdom of indigenous peoples. It makes sense to me in so many ways. Where there is some old belief left the land is still intact, or being fought for. Where it is not, opportunism threatens to take all that it can. I fully agree that in the modern world we are rich in the comfort and convenience of technology that industry has brought us. Like many who are fortunate, I enjoy a comfortable

dwelling and improved communication and transport. But I feel I must re-evaluate my 'desire' for such luxuries in my new-found knowledge of their real cost.

One of the many things that I have learned in the Arctic is that every one of our actions has an effect elsewhere, whether it's environmental or financial, in terms of who is supporting development here and who stands to gain the most. Is my bank ethical? Where is my pension invested? What is the knock-on effect of everything I buy? Do I need to eat meat and fish everyday? What is my impact on the environment? Where is everything coming from? Am I respecting the planet, and can I do more?

We are each responsible for our own actions – we should all be the change we want to see – but, for my own part, I believe awareness is also the key. I appreciate the contradictions of travelling the world to create so large a project, a book and films, but things like this must help in their own way, surely? I hope my journey can stimulate debate and encourage an interest in this place and its people.

The Arctic has become the showcase for the effects of climate change, the window onto a troubled world, perhaps seemingly far from our everyday concerns. If we have achieved anything with our project, with this short journey among the

THIS PAGE: Gold prospectors' cabins hug the foreshore at Nome, Alaska.
OVERLEAF: My view of the Arctic has matured greatly during this past summer. Though I fear for its future, my respect for the people of the Arctic has never been greater.
FOLLOWING PAGES: I owe much to the many people I have met on my travels, including my companions from Qaanaaq where my journey began.

people of the North, it must be to have helped others recognize that what happens in the Arctic affects all of us. The evidence was there throughout my journey. Just as the warming Arctic opens the door to all sorts of current problems, it can also be the area to prove how we can meet these challenges.

Today I think society faces a fundamental choice with the Arctic. Do we continue industrial expansion into one of the last wild areas of the world, extracting the billions of tons of fossil carbon energy there, further degrading the region and the global environment? Or, do we strive to find another way, a more sustainable future for this remarkable place? It is only if we choose wisely that I believe the future of coming generations will be assured. The polar bears may be long gone.

Have ever you heard of the Land of Beyond,
That dreams at the gates of the day?
Alluring it lies at the skirts of the skies,
And ever so far away;
Alluring it calls: O ye the yoke galls,
And ye of the trail overfond,
With saddle and pack, by paddle and track,
Let's go to the Land of Beyond!

Have ever you stood where the silences brood,
And vast the horizons begin,
At the dawn of the day to behold far away
The goal you would strive for and win?
Yet ah! in the night when you gain to the height,
With the vast pool of heaven star-spawned,
Afar and agleam, like a valley of dream,
Still mocks you a Land of Beyond.

Robert Service, 1912

ACKNOWLEDGEMENTS

This book, and the films that it accompanies, tells the story of my journey in the Arctic during the course of one bright summer. On these often difficult, yet exciting, journeys I am sustained by the knowledge that the people I'm travelling with, and those supporting me at home, are all committed to helping me express my understanding of the world and our place in it. I do this for the benefit of everyone.

So many creative and talented people have joined together to ensure this is a success, a fact that has made the whole thing such an enjoyable and satisfying experience. Sure, some times were tough and the work was hard. But mostly it has been a real joy, a privilege.

But the people involved in the films, or the book, are only half the story. In many ways the equal, if not greater, thanks must go to those hundreds of people I've met on my journey through the Arctic. Many of their names are missing from this list and most will remain strangers to me. At other times, I have been welcomed into people's lives. I've shared their dreams and learned more about their world. For this I will be forever grateful.

This series was commissioned by Charlotte Moore and Janice Hadlow at the BBC. Thanks to them and everyone else there who has helped me along the way. The series was executive produced for the BBC by Nick Shearman with precision and care and I am grateful for his hard work.

These films, indeed much of my career so far, owe most to Steve Robinson, Executive Producer of Arctic. I know I can be infuriating but I do love you dearly. I hope we have many more films ahead of us.

At Indus, the rest of the team help and improve me in so many different ways. I thank Gwenllian Hughes and Rick Mabey, Heads of Production, in particular. Leona Cowley, Production Manager, Melanie Guinee and Emma Haskins simply run our lives while we're away and hardly sleep through worry half the time.

To the film guys on the ground, who lend me their vision and expertise: James Smith, Series Producer and director of the Greenland and Norway films; Robert Sullivan, Director of Canada and Alaska; and Gavin Searle, Director of Siberia. Gents, you all know me better than most. Thank you for letting me rant, thanks for humouring me. Thank you for listening and then packaging me into an acceptable format for public consumption. Yours is a difficult job and I'm very lucky you are all so brilliant.

To our Assistant Producers Vicky Hinners and David Marks, and researcher Sara Moralioglu, quite the best field team, who shaped my films well by finding amazing contributors, locations, and generally organizing everything for me when it all went to pot. To our fixers Rob Toohey, John Markel, Ken and Tandy Wallack, Lena Yakoleva and assistant Hannah Gosney who all offered invaluable local knowledge, setting us in the direction of interesting stories.

To Johnny Rogers and Richard Farish our cameramen for their extraordinary talent. Thanks to our talented soundman Zubin Sarosh, my trusted travelling companion, who also took the majority of the super photographs that appear in this book.

And to our film Editors, Alex Boyle, Gwynfor Llewellyn and Peter Brownlee. You guys make me sound like I know what I'm talking about. I'm not sure how you weave your magic, but keep it up please. It's amazing and I don't deserve it.

There are others to acknowledge: Richard Moss, the guys at Mwnci, Greg Provan, Steve Castle, Jason Gibbs, Mark Young, Owain Elidir, Paul Nicholas, Nick Dacey, and many others too.

In Greenland, the communities of Qaanaaq and Uummannaq, in particular my friends Rasmus Avike, Mads Ole Kristiensen, Toku Oshima, Paulos Simiaq, Tobias, Adolph. I thank our translator David Qujaukitsoq, Mads Norlund at Greenland Tourism, Hans Jensen, and David Qujaukitsoq. I thank Tim Daffern and Nils Trausser for access and explanation of the Black Angel Mine. To the wonderful Ann Andreasen, Ole Jørgen Hammeken, the staff and the brave young people of the Children's Home in Uummannaq. I wish you all well.

In Canada, I really enjoyed my time with the people of Old Crow and Fort Chipewyan. In particular, noble Stephen Frost, Margaret Frost, Peter Frost; Robert Williams, Donald Russell, Robert Kaikauchik, Robert Grandjambe. To honest Patricia Grandjambe, who let me ride in her truck; Steve Courtoreille, Edward Marten and to Rita Vermillion for giving me a drum. I use it regularly. To Dr John O'Connor and the patients in his care. My thoughts are with you all as you struggle to overcome the difficulties of having industry so close. And Chief Jim Boucher, his staff, and members of the Fort McKay First Nation.

In Siberia, special thanks to: Alexander 'Kulan' Sergeevich Artemiev and his extended family. We will meet again, I'm sure. To Sergei Lukin, horseman of Sakkyryr, and his family; anthropologist Dr Florian Stammler and his wife Anna Stammler-Gossmann, our translator; Sasha Ivanov and Aitalina Ivanova; Innokentii Ammossov and his wife Nadezhda for her cakes; the team from brigade number 8, especially Vasili Popov, Piotr Konstantinov, Yegor Sleptsov; and staff at the Arctic Centre, University of Lapland.

In Alaska, in Prince William Sound, we are grateful to Tim and Berry Cabana; in Nome, hats off to gold-guru Steve Philips and son Spencer, whose company I enjoyed greatly and with whom I learned much and enjoyed 'discussing' politics long into each night. And a warm and genuine thanks to Marie and Eddie Rexford, Flora and Eddie Junior; Bruce Inglangasak; Charlie Rexford, George Kalaik; James and Glenda Lampe, their crew and kids, Mayor Annie Tikluk, and the community of Katovik.

Lastly, in Norway, my travels and my understanding of the changes happening there were greatly enhanced by Professor Kim Holmén, Research Director of the

Norwegian Polar Institute; Communications Director Gunn Sissel Jaklin; Max Konig; Sebastien Barrault; Nick Cox; Svein Andersen of FilmCamp; Jason Roberts, film-maker in Longyearbyen; Jonas Karlsbakk and staff at the Norwegian Barents Secretariat; Professor Timo Karjalainen of the Finnish Forest Research Institute; Dr Andrew Gromstev, forestry expert at the Russian Academy of Sciences; Eva Therese Jenssen and other staff at the University Centre in Svalbard; and French glaciologist Dr Madeleine Griselin and her colleagues. I thank the Oskal Siida, especially Johan Isak and Danel, my guides in the hills above Tromsø. Also, Johan Anders, Ole Mathis, Nils Ole, Isak Toure, Toure Anders and Lars Thomas. I truly wish you all good fortune in keeping your traditions and values alive. We all have much to learn from you.

Deep in the Russian forest, Ivan Petrovich Ilyin, Ksenia Yartseva, and the people of Nyukhcha Village; Alexei Ivanovich Kychyov who does so much for the trees; and Schultz Yekaterina Baikalova. Katya, thank you for your time, and your potion.

Back in Britain, I'm so pleased to now work with the fantastic team at Anova Books: Polly Powell, Jonathan White, Komal Patel, Georgina Hewitt and, in particular, John Lee and Alison Moss who were crucial to making this happen. Good job, guys.

To my friend and ghostwriter Dr Huw Lewis-Jones, who did the lion's share of writing for this project, often with little material to work with and always patiently under tough deadlines. Without you this book would not exist. So, thank you for your tolerance and understanding of what I'm trying to say, for your gentle skill at shaping my diary, and for giving me words when I lacked them. I'm super happy with everything you've done and I know we've all benefitted from your eloquence and intellect. Thank you, mate.

To my family and friends, not least Madeline, who still picks up the pieces of my disorganized life and looks after my finca in the sun and, not to forget, Dorian the Dude and Chingis the Cheerful, when I'm away. Sorry, and thank you always.

To our dear friend Sam Organ who sadly passed away on our first day of filming, who we all miss so dearly, and to whom I dedicate this book.

And, finally, to a new friend – the Arctic. I've visited you a number of times in my life so far and I humbly admit that my words have not always been complimentary. But, having now finally got to know you better I hereby admit I was utterly wrong. Beneath a frosty exterior, lies the warmest of all hearts, and I've been lucky to experience this now. I am sorry how we are treating you and I hope, from the depths of my soul, that we may realize the error of our ways. Forgive us.

Bruce Parry
Ibiza, November 2010

INDEX

Figures in *italics* indicate captions.